CHILDREN OF THE SUN

Japanese tradition holds that the Sun Goddess, Amaterasu Omikami, is the ancestral divinity of the Japanese Imperial Family. She is said to have been born of Izanagi, the creative divinity of Japan.

Children
of the SUN
MICHIO KITAHARA

THE JAPANESE AND THE OUTSIDE WORLD

Paul Norbury Publications
Sandgate, Folkestone, England

CHILDREN OF THE SUN
The Japanese and the Outside World

First published 1989 by
PAUL NORBURY PUBLICATIONS
Knoll House, 35 The Crescent
Sandgate, Folkestone, Kent, England CT20 3EE

ISBN 0-904404-68-4

British Library Cataloguing in Publication Data

Kitahara, Michio, *1937 –*
   Children of the Sun: The
   Japanese and the Outside
   World.
   1. Japanese culture — sociological
   perspectives
   I. Title
   306'.0952

ISBN 0-904404-68-4

Set in Goudy Old Style Roman 11 on 12½ point by Visual Typesetting, Harrow, Middlesex
Printed in Great Britain by A. Wheaton & Co. Ltd., Exeter

Till Ulla Davidsson,
som accepterar mitt liv
som orangutang

Contents

Acknowledgements

Acknowledgement is gratefully made to the following copyright holders for permission to reproduce materials from my journal articles in rewritten forms; Duncker and Humblot GmbH for 'Japanese Attitudes Toward the Chinese and the Koreans in History,' *Sociologia Internationalis* 25, 1987; JAI Press, Inc. for 'Commodore Perry and the Japanese,' *Symbolic Interaction* 9, 1986; Otto Harrassowitz for 'The Rise of Four Mottoes in Japan before and after the Meiji Restoration,' *Journal of Asian History* 20, 1986; E. J. Brill for 'The Western Impact on Japanese Racial Self-Image,' *Journal of Developing Societies* 3, 1987; © Gordon and Breach, Science Publishers, S.A. for 'Psychoanalytic Aspects of Japanese Militarism,' *International Interactions* 12, 1985; Avenue Publishing Co. for 'Japanese Responses to the Defeat in World War II,' *International Journal of Social Psychiatry* 30, 1984; Pi Gamma Mu, Inc. for 'Douglas MacArthur as a Father Figure in Occupied Japan after World War II,' *International Social Science Review* 63, 1988; William S. Hall Psychiatric Institute for 'Psychoanalytic Themes in Japanese Literature,' *Psychiatric Forum* 13, 1984-85; and Ray B. Browne for 'Popular Culture in Japan,' *Journal of Popular Culture* 17, 1983.

Preface

I THOUGHT about the ideas expressed in this book for many years. But at the same time, I also thought that it would be very difficult to get such ideas published. In 1980, I finally wrote a short, poorly organised paper, which happened to be read by Dr Howard F. Stein. To my surprise, he saw certain values in my approach and encouraged me to revise and expand it. The new version was later published in the *Journal of Psychoanalytic Anthropology*, which Dr Stein edited.

After the publication of this article, I received encouraging letters and comments from various scholars in different fields, including psychiatry and psychology. These reactions encouraged me to publish further 'linking' articles in professional journals in the United States and Europe. These, too, attracted favourable comments, and I finally decided to publish a book for the general reader by avoiding professional jargon as much as possible. Thus, without Dr Stein's initial encouragement, I would never have written *Children of the Sun*.

In the preparation of this book other scholars also offered me encouragement, comments, and suggestions. They are, in alphabetical order, Drs John M. Johnson, Stephen Salaff, Melford E. Spiro, and Benjamin Tong. To me, their sympathetic help meant much more than they can imagine.

I am very fortunate to have Mr Paul Norbury as my publisher. His keen insight into things Japanese helped me to clarify and improve the discussions in the book significantly. To all these persons, I would like to express my sincere gratitude.

MICHIO KITAHARA

Partille, Sweden

2 March 1988

Introduction

THERE ARE many books on Japan. The subjects treated are legion — from cooking, literature, judo and the economy to history, the family, the arts, and so on. When you consider this great range of topics, you could be forgiven for thinking that there is really no room for yet another book about Japan. It goes without saying, therefore, that if I have decided to add one more to the list, there must be a very good reason. Let me try to explain.

Gradually, I began to realise that some aspects of Japanese culture and behaviour could be explained psychoanalytically. Of course, psychoanalysis is a very broad field, and it is more than a method for treating depressed or emotionally disturbed people. Some concepts of psychoanalysis are applicable to normal people in their everyday life, especially when they are placed in a crisis situation. My assumption, therefore, is that if we look at the Japanese and their culture from this perspective, we can consistently (or predictably) understand many of the phenomena and peculiarities associated with the Japanese. Psychoanalysis can provide us with an insight that will enable us to comprehend Japanese culture in a way that the study of, say, Japanese economic growth or politics or even literature will never do.

For example, by using some psychoanalytical concepts, I can answer a wide variety of questions and queries, such as: In the eighth century, why did some Japanese refer to Japan as 'China'? Why could Commodore Perry succeed in opening Japan after many other westerners had failed to do so? Why did Japan become westernised? Why did Japanese export copy-cat products after westernisation? During World War II, why did they refer to Americans and Britons as 'devil-beasts'? Why could General

MacArthur successfully administer occupied Japan after World War II? Why did some Japanese teenagers pretend to be Japanese Americans after the War? Why did some Japanese seriously want to make Japan the 49th state of the US? Why do they ridicule short-legged Japanese? Why do some Japanese undergo nose-heightening plastic surgery? Why do Japanese, especially girls, smile and giggle when a westerner talks to them?

These and many more questions are answered in this book from a psychoanalytical point of view. Of course, I am not saying that all of Japanese culture can be explained psychoanalytically. That is absurd. But I do say that psychoanalysis offers a very valid and important way of understanding Japanese culture. I wrote *Children of the Sun* with this particular focus because nobody has attempted to do so before.

However, in order to avoid misunderstanding or encourage accusation, I must clarify my position here. I am not saying that a culture has its own 'mind.' It is always individuals who think and respond psychoanalytically. To state my position more accurately: my considerations and analysis concern the psychoanalytical responses that are to be found *within* Japanese society. I am well aware of the fact that, like any other living species, *Homo sapiens* manifests infinite variations in thought and behaviour. Naturally, there are Japanese who think and behave in deviant ways. It is also possible that some Japanese respond to a certain event psychoanalytically, while others are not aware of such an event. The Japanese would never think and feel exactly alike — nor, for that matter, would the French or the English or the Chinese.

Nevertheless, it is also conceivable that when the thought and action of a certain Japanese is accepted, sympathised with, or acclaimed, a significant portion of the members of Japanese culture think and feel similarly. This assumption would apply to popular or influential political thinkers, journalists, or novelists. Indeed, if a person is too deviant in his or her thought or behaviour, he or she is likely to be ridiculed or ignored. This precept is borne out by the axiom that 'the protruding nail shall be hammered flat.'

A good example of what I mean here is the case of Mishima Yukio. As a novelist, he was widely read and acclaimed in Japan, but as a political activist, he was considered too deviant and the majority of Japanese could not understand him. When he committed ritual suicide, in November 1970, his deviance became even more extreme and most Japanese simply sneered. I think it is quite proper to refer to Mishima's novels in order to discuss Japanese culture, but it is totally inadequate and even grotesque to infer the nature of Japanese culture by studying his suicidal behaviour, as one American psychiatrist has done. In this book, I intend to discuss the thoughts and behaviour patterns of those Japanese who in my opinion represent the significant portion of the members of Japanese culture at a certain stage in Japanese history.

•　　•　　•

To some readers, terms such as psychology, psychoanalysis, and psychiatry may sound alike and confusing, and a brief explanation of these terms at this point may be useful. *Psychology* can be defined as the study of mind and behaviour and is very broad and comprehensive in meaning. Psychologists study both human beings and animals — individually or collectively. They can be normal or abnormal. An unfortunate fact about contemporary English usage is that we tend to use the word 'psychology' instead of 'mind', and 'psychological' instead of 'mental'. In these situations, 'psychology' and 'psychological' merely mean 'mind' and 'mental'.

Psychoanalysis is mainly concerned with mild or serious mental disorders among humans, which are assumed to be caused by some kind of social experience. A psychoanalyst is also interested in treating mentally disturbed people, but he or she may or may not be a medical doctor. *Psychiatry* is a branch of medicine that deals with mental disorders, and psychoanalysis may be applied for the purpose of diagnosis and treatment, in addition to medication.

Although I am going to discuss the Japanese and their culture psychoanalytically in this book, psychoanalysis is actually a very broad field, and I can discuss only the ways Japanese respond to threats in terms of the psychoanalytical perspective. In psychoanalysis, it is assumed that a person responds to a threat in one way or another by manipulating his thoughts in his mind in order to defend himself; these methods of defence are called, quite appropriately, I think, 'defence mechanisms'. I am going to refer to a total of nine defence mechanisms in this book, and among them, 'identification with the aggressor' is the most important.

A detailed discussion of the defence mechanisms is offered in the Appendix at the back of the book, but for the sake of simplicity and ready access a brief explanation of these defence mechanisms is provided at the end of this Introduction.

The book contains many Japanese names, which are set out according to Japanese convention, that is, the family name first. As in China and Korea, as well as in Hungary and historic Finland, the given name comes after the family name in Japan. For example, I refer to a man who lived around the Meiji Restoration of 1868 as Saigo Takamori, because Saigo is his family name.

Finally, I would like to add a few words regarding my English. I wrote this book in English because English is the most widely understood language in the world. But like most European languages, English has some awkward characteristics. I shall not go into details here by giving examples, but one problem consistently exists. And that is the problem of gender. I know full well that a 'person' can be either male or female, and it is better to write like this: 'A person denies the reality of the objective world. He or she refuses to admit that a disturbing fact does exist.' But it is awkward to have to write 'he or she', 'his or her' or 'him or her'. I tried to avoid using the third person singular form and the expression 'man' in order to refer to 'people' or 'we.' But when I am obliged to use the word 'person,' I often follow with 'his' or 'him' in order to avoid awkwardness. I happen to be a male, but this practice does not necessarily reveal a tendency towards 'male chauvinism'.

The Nine Defence Mechanisms Referred To In This Book

Denial:
Refusal to admit the reality of the objective world.

Displacement:
Releasing one's energy through a substitute channel.

Identification with the aggressor:
Placing oneself in the position of the threatening person through imagination and understanding, and looking at the world through his eyes.

Intellectualisation:
Explanation of a disturbing phenomenon by using abstract, scholarly words without involving emotion.

Isolation:
Elimination of emotions and feelings from one's thought.

Projection:
Attributing one's own characteristic to another person.

Rationalisation:
A superficial explanation which makes one's behaviour justifiable and plausible.

Reaction formation:
A reversal of thought and feeling.

Regression:
Going back to an earlier stage in one's life, such as an adult becoming childish.

1 China and Korea and Japan

THE CHINESE developed their own writing system centuries ahead of the Japanese. Indeed, while the Japanese were still a relatively primitive people, the Chinese had already seen the rise and fall of civilisations. Moreover, the Japanese were unable to invent their own writing system by themselves. They began to write in the fifth century by borrowing the Chinese writing system. The Japanese later modified and simplified the Chinese characters, but the dominance and importance of the Chinese characters throughout Japanese history is indisputable. As a matter of fact, in today's world of electronics, the Japanese are rather pleased to have developed word processors for the Chinese characters.

In order to learn about Japan before they began to write about themselves, therefore, the official records of the Chinese dynasties are the only written sources. In China, after the fall of a dynasty, its history was written by the officials of the next dynasty. Such a work required time and hard work. For example, it took 60 years to complete the history of the Ming Dynasty (1368-1644).

Japan's Inferior Position in East-Asian History

The first statement regarding the Japanese appears in documents about the Chien Han Dynasty (202 BC-8 AD). But the description is very brief, merely stating that the Japanese exist in the east. The Chinese wrote that the barbarians in the east, namely the Japanese, were docile and obedient by nature and that they were different from other barbarians in this regard.

Much later in time, when Japan was eager to absorb the advanced culture of the Tang Dynasty (618 AD-907 AD) the official document of the dynasty described the five barbaric countries in the east, including Japan. According to these records, two different names were used in referring to the Japanese islands, and 628 characters were used in the description. This is much less than the number of characters devoted to the description of the three countries on the Korean peninsula; for them, 9901 characters were used.

Although the culture of the Tang Dynasty was very important to and a considerable influence on the Japanese, this meager description suggests that the Chinese did not think Japan sufficiently important to write much about it. In any event, on an international level, Japan was likely to be very insignificant. The power relationship between China and Japan is clearly stated in this document. For example, in 631 AD, Japan sent a diplomatic delegation to the Emperor of China and offered a tribute. The Emperor felt sorry for the Japanese because they had to travel such a long way, and, as a result, he made it unnecessary for them to make the trip every year.

After the decline of the Tang Dynasty, the contact between China and Japan was much reduced. Yet until the middle of the nineteenth century, the way the Chinese looked at and understood Japan had been very much the same. Japan was a subordinate country and the Japanese were one of the barbaric peoples. The Chinese looked at Japanese culture as a modified version of Chinese culture, and they tended to see Japanese cultural traits as derived from Chinese culture.

Some of the Japanese cultural traits which the Chinese think are of Chinese origin are: women's hairdo; the pillow; the practice of carrying the baby on the back; *gagaku* (music played in the imperial household and the Shinto shrines); the *tokonoma* (the alcove in the room); the way to sit; *geta* (clogs); *koshimaki* (women's underwear); *kakebuton* (bedclothes); cakes; tea; *goh* (board game using stones); *shogi* (chess); the practice of employing a maid at home; the way of washing the head; the *kimono*; the way of carrying the tray at eye level before serving a meal to a guest; and the practice of the host drinking *saké* first before serving it to the guest.

Whether or not these beliefs are true is another matter. These are spontaneous observations by Chinese travellers and Chinese residents in Japan. But their observations do reflect the centuries-old Chinese belief that Japanese culture is a modified version of Chinese culture. Of course, there are many other traits of Chinese origin which are not mentioned here.

The extent of China's impact on Japanese culture can be easily seen in the lives of ordinary folk both today and in the past. A good example is the enormous heritage of Japanese proverbs and maxims which impinge on daily life but which are actually of Chinese origin. Many *rakugo*, or funny stories and jokes for the masses narrated by *rakugoka*, or professional story-tellers, quote these proverbs and maxims. In this way, merchants, carpenters, artisans, and peasants in the past and white-collar and blue-collar workers after the Meiji Restoration were exposed to Chinese culture.

At least during certain periods of history, the countries on the Korean peninsula were also very important to the Japanese. According to one study by a Japanese scholar, Japan held the lowest position in the ranking of the nations in east Asia in the early historic period. The countries on the Korean peninsula were below China, but Japan was even below them. For example, in the fifth century, Japan ranked below Paekche, and in the eighth century below Silla. In the eyes of the Japanese, the countries on the peninsula were the mediators of the advanced cultures in China and were also the holders of advanced cultures themselves. Printed holy scriptures, for example, from the Korean peninsula were highly valued by the upper class Japanese.

Japanese Admiration of the Cultures of the Continent

In order to absorb the benefit of the advanced continental cultures, Japan began to send students to China. This was done most actively during the Tang Dynasty, and between 618 AD and 906 AD, 27 groups of students were sent. The total number of Japanese on each occasion ranged from 99 to 615, and about a half of them were rowers. The other half consisted of government officials, interpreters, medical doctors, musicians, and tradesmen, in addition to a large number of students. They usually sailed in four ships. The technology of building ships was primitive, and they could not exploit available winds effectively for navigation. As a result, many people were needed to row the ships!

For a small and primitive country, to send students like this must have been a heavy burden. But the objective was very important to the Japanese, and they continued to send students even when some of them were exploited and robbed by Chinese officials. There were also the problems of coping with pirates on the high seas and the ever-present danger of storms and tempests. We are obliged to acknowledge, therefore, a very strong motivating force on the part of the Japanese.

Indeed, among the Japanese, their envy and admiration of the cultures on the continent is clearly seen in their literature. For example, in the *Kojiki*, the first recorded history of Japan written in 712 AD, there are two references to Korea which can be seen as expressions of envy. In this work, a god comes down to Japan from heaven and says to his two subordinates: 'This land is facing towards Korea... Therefore this is a good land.[1] Korea is also described as a country of gold, silver, and jewels. Another major work, completed in 720 AD and entitled *Nihon Shoki*, recounts how Silla has more wealth than Japan.

Similarly, in *Eiga Monogatari*, one of the representative works of the Heian Period (781-1185), the author describes Japanese who dressed up on a formal occasion: 'This is not unique to Japan. In Korea or China it must be just like this.' In *Imakagami*, another major work of the same period, musicians played music in a moving boat in front of Emperor Goreizei. The people watching the event thought it was beautiful and said to each other: 'In China it would be just like this.' Later in the same work, after watching ten dancers who performed in front of the Emperor, the author wrote: 'We felt as if we were witnessing a dance by Chinese ladies.'

In these descriptions, anything refined, beautiful, or sophisticated was considered to be similar to a cultural standard epitomised in China or Korea. The same attitude can also be seen with regard to scholarly achievements. For example, in *Daiki*, another work from the Heian Period, the author describes two gentlemen who engaged in a scholarly debate. After the debate, one of them commended the other highly and said: 'I apologise for assuming that you are a mere novice. You are extraordinarily gifted. You are already beyond the first-rate scholars of this country. This country is not suitable for your talent. Even in China, people like you are quite rare.'

In these examples, it is clear that the Chinese and Korean standards were the goal to achieve, and when a Japanese reached or came close to it, he or she was commended and admired. I should add that most of these works were written in Chinese.

Identification with the Aggressor

Since it is impossible to psychoanalyse people who lived many centuries ago, we can only speculate how they actually thought and felt. I suggest that the Japanese identified with the peoples on the continent in order to deal with their inferior position. By means of identification, they tried to reduce their fear and feeling of inferiority towards China and the Korean countries. As you will recall, through identification, one imagines oneself to be somebody else and tries to think and feel like this other person. Successful identification means that one comes to think and feel just like that person. If we apply this concept to the Japanese, we might infer that many upper-class Japanese and intellectuals identified with the upper-class people and intellectuals on the continent and thought and felt like them. These Japanese looked at themselves as if they were the same as the continental peoples.

Indeed, there is clear evidence that some Japanese conceived of Japan as a 'miniature China.' A study of these past Japanese attitudes and practices would be either inconceivable or offensive to many present-day Japanese; yet it is a fact that all the relevant records were written by Japanese.

For example, both in 699 AD and 722 AD, the Japanese imperial household was referred to as '*chugoku*.' The word '*chugoku*' was originally a Chinese word meaning 'the country in the centre.' This of course refers to China, signifying that China is the centre of civilisation according to the way the Chinese looked at and understood the world. But the Japanese borrowed the Chinese word and referred to their own imperial household as 'China.' Similarly, in the first collection of poems written by Japanese in the Chinese language and published in 751 AD, Japan was again referred to as 'China.' This practice of referring to Japan as 'China' clearly already existed in the early part of Japan's Nara Period (710 AD-784 AD).

This 'China perspective' persisted throughout the centuries among Japanese scholars. For example, Yamaga Soko wrote in the seventeenth century: '*Chugoku* is a land superior to the other lands and its people are superior. [Therefore] our land is a divine land.' Of course, Yamaga did not write in English; I have translated his sentences from the Chinese. You may accuse me of misinterpreting and misrepresenting what he wrote, but specialists agree that Yamaga is referring to Japan as 'China' in this context.

Asami Keisai, another scholar in the seventeenth and eighteenth centuries, wrote: '*Chugoku* is the most important country for me, because *Chugoku* is my native country.' He was not born in China, of course; he spent his entire life in Japan. Thinking like this was not limited to a few unusual scholars. Indeed in 1828, Yamazaki Yoshinari made the criticism that in Japan, 'study' meant the study of Chinese writings and the most learned scholars were those who knew only Chinese works.

Identification with the Chinese was expressed in an absurd way by some scholars. For example, some Japanese began to reinterpret Chinese history in terms of a Japanese context. According to this approach, eminent figures in Chinese history were believed to have been in Japan, and various events in Chinese history and legend were thought to have taken place in Japan. For example, Confucius came to Japan with 70 disciples in a junk.

Often a scholar worshipped China as the centre of civilisation and by assuming the Chinese point of view, considered the Japanese as barbarians. Dogen, a Buddhist priest who went to China in 1223 as a student and stayed there for four years is a well-known example. He idealised China and considered Japan to be a barbaric and uncivilised country.

Another well-known scholar was Ogyu Sorai in the eighteenth century. He called himself a 'barbarian in the east of China,' and he changed his name to one which sounded more Chinese. He believed that the Japanese could not create a civilisation; only the Chinese could. In his opinion, successful scholars could only emerge in China. He was said to be very happy when he moved to a new home because its location was a little closer to China!

A man like Ogyu Sorai was not at all unusual. Indeed, during the Edo Period when the Japanese were not allowed to travel abroad, there were scholars who travelled from Edo (present-day Tokyo) to Nagasaki. It was a trip of more than 700 miles; mostly on foot. The reason for this pilgrimage was to come closer to China physically. When a China worshipper reaches this stage, his behaviour becomes religious.

Identification with China as a Means to Deal with Korea

By identifying with the Chinese, the Japanese tried to deal with their sense of inferiority towards and fear of the Chinese. China was a huge, powerful, and very advanced country and was the centre of civilisation. By identifying with the Chinese and by trying to think and feel like the Chinese, the Japanese could look at the world from the standpoint of a huge, powerful, and advanced country. When successful, they could forget about the reality, while the reality was that of a weak and underdeveloped people. In this sense, identification with the aggressor as a defence mechanism was useful.

Another valuable by-product of identification with the Chinese meant that the Japanese could also deal with their feeling of inferiority towards the peoples on the Korean peninsula. In 703 AD, when a diplomatic delegation from Silla arrived, the Japanese Imperial Household made an official statement saying that the King of Silla was a barbarian king, but he could be considered equivalent to the beloved child of the Emperor of Japan. This was the first written statement by the Japanese revealing the fact that they looked down on the Koreans. As you will recall, Japan occupied the lowest position in the international ranking of the nations in east Asia, and this was certainly true when this statement was made in 703 AD. Therefore, it is clear that this statement is not in agreement with the objective facts of the period. By making an official statement like this, the Japanese were trying to deal with their inferior international position defensively.

From the Chinese point of view, however, the relative positions of Silla and Japan were not completely irreversible. After all, both were low-status countries, and they were both probably totally irrelevant to the Chinese. In 754 AD, at a diplomatic meeting in the Chinese Imperial Court, the Japanese delegate was assigned to a seat which was lower in ranking than the seat for the delegate from Silla. The Japanese strongly protested, and finally the seats for the two delegates were exchanged.

In a situation like this, there was room for a low-status nation such as Japan to reduce its unpleasant feelings by diplomatic efforts as well as by defence mechanisms. Actually, I am not at all sure whether or not the complaint over the seating arrangements at a diplomatic meeting should be called a 'diplomatic effort', but this well-known incident suggests that in terms of international common sense, Japan occupied a position lower than that of Silla.

What we can say in this context is that the Japanese identified with the Chinese and looked at other peoples from the Chinese point of view. The Japanese tried to convince themselves that they were better than the peoples on the Korean peninsula; they thought and felt like the Chinese, and in order to substantiate their reasoning, they had to see this in reality by exchanging seats at a diplomatic meeting.

Japanese actions that were designed to reinforce their perceived superior status became increasingly apparent. For example, the Japanese began to discriminate against and to oppress the immigrants from Silla, and historically, this phenomenon began to appear in the 830s AD. Even naturalised Koreans were expelled from Japan and they were forbidden to re-enter the country.

Psychoanalytically, here are both projection and displacement. Why? Because the Japanese knew that Silla was a low-status country. Nevertheless, the Chinese evaluated Silla more favourably than Japan, for example, by giving Silla a better seat at the diplomatic meeting. This was irritating and frustrating to the Japanese. They said to themselves: 'Silla is a low-status country. Why are they better than us?' They envied Silla by being evaluated more favourably by China, but envy does not solve the problem. Japan continued to exist as a lower-status nation than Silla. That was a fact — an international fact decided by China.

When envy does not solve the problem, the possibility of a defence mechanism emerges. By means of a psychological manipulation of thought, the Japanese tried to defend their miserable position. And the defence mechanism was projection. First, envy was changed into hatred. 'We envy them' became 'We hate them.' By means of projection, the hatred on the part of the Japanese was projected onto the people of Silla. 'We hate them' became 'They hate us.' The people from Silla were considered undesirable and dangerous and unwanted. Projection was complete. Negative attitudes towards them paved the way for action.

The action here is displacement, which was expressed in

the form of discrimination and oppression. Displacement was possible because Silla was a weak, low-status country. The Japanese could even release their anger and frustration resulting from their intercourse with the Chinese. No matter how the Japanese became angry and frustrated because of the way the Chinese handled them, they could not attack the Chinese because the Chinese were too powerful. To deal with the anger and frustration, however, Silla was a suitable target country. Instead of attacking China, the Japanese could attack Silla. This was also displacement.

Indeed, through time, anti-Korean arrogance began to emerge in Japan. Korea was finally invaded twice towards the end of the sixteenth century. In 1789, a Japanese scholar wrote that Korea had been a subordinate country for a long time in history — a view that was commonly held by the Japanese during the Edo Period (1600-1868).

When Europeans, and later Americans, began to appear as the peoples with more advanced technology and military power, the Japanese were faced with a problem similar to the one they had had earlier with the Chinese and other nearby continental peoples. Through the realisation that the westerners were more powerful than the Chinese, the Japanese identified with the westerners. The westerners took over the prestigious top echelon position in the minds of the Japanese. The Japanese this time began to look at the world through the eyes of the West, and this time, *both* the Chinese *and* the Koreans became the objects of projection and displacement. It is interesting to realise that the Japanese always identify with the most powerful people at any particular time and then try to look at the world defensively through the eyes of that people. This is the Japanese way of life. We shall come back to this point in more detail later.

2 Commodore Perry: A Drama of Power Display

ALTHOUGH JAPAN stopped sending students to China in the ninth century, the continent's cultural influences continued. Since Japan consists of islands, the Japanese were relatively isolated from other peoples, and they could remain largely undisturbed by outside forces. The only exception was two attempted invasions by the Mongols in 1274 and 1281. But the Mongols did not occupy Japan, and the threat they posed did not exist long enough to make a significant impact on Japanese culture. At least it is fair to say that we fail to recognise any Mongolian influence on Japanese culture.

The first recorded contact between Japan and the West took place in 1543 when a Portuguese ship drifted up to one of the smaller islands of Japan. After this, Portuguese and Spanish missionaries and merchants began to come to Japan. At first, they were welcomed by the Japanese, because they brought western innovations and curious items of interest. But more and more westerners followed in their path, and the shogunate (military regime headed by a shogun) realised that western religion and ideology challenged the *status quo* and were therefore unacceptable; consequently, in 1639 the shogunate decided to terminate all relations with foreigners and implemented final expulsion orders. However, they allowed the Chinese and the Dutch to remain. But after 1641 the Dutch were confined to a small island called Deshima within Nagasaki harbour, and after 1688 the Chinese were confined to a special quarter in Nagasaki.

The Japanese were succeful in maintaining this seclusion policy for more than 200 years. But in the meantime, Europe was entering the age of expansionism and colonialism, and Japan began to feel the intensity of their threat more and more. For example, in 1808, an English man-o'-war with a Dutch flag illegally entered the port of Nagasaki and blackmailed Dutch residents on Deshima island. In response to this incident, the Tokugawa government enforced their get-tough policy by ordering the expulsion of all foreign ships from Japanese territorial waters. The law became effective in 1825 and remained in force for 17 years.

During Japan's seclusion, the Dutch were the only Europeans who were allowed to trade with Japan, and from time to time, the Japanese were informed about the major events in the world by the Dutch. In 1844, in a letter to the Tokugawa government, Wilhelm II, King of Holland, informed the shogunate that China had been forced to terminate its seclusion policy as a result of the Opium War, and he also explained the military advances that were taking place among the western nations. Accordingly, he advised Japan to terminate her seclusion policy forthwith and come to terms with the new world order. Japan rejected this advice a year later in 1845.

In 1846, an American Navy official demanded the establishment of diplomatic relations with Japan, but this was turned down. The Americans did not give up, however. They decided to send a fleet to Japan to make the same request. In 1851, the Americans notified the Dutch about their decision and asked for their cooperation.

Presentation of a Drama

The famous Commodore Perry expedition to Japan should be understood with this historical background in mind. His mission was to open Japan; a task other westerners had failed to achieve. But Perry was determined to accomplish the mission assigned to him. In a letter to the US Secretary of the Navy written in 1852, Perry says: 'I feel confident that in the end the great object in view will be effected....I feel a strong confidence of success...It should be, under whatever circumstances, accomplished.'

In order to make his expedition successful, Perry read many books on Japan in order to obtain a clear idea of who the Japanese were. For example, in his diary, he wrote that the duplicity of the Japanese was well known. Perry wrote a very detailed diary throughout his expedition, which is enjoyable and at times amusing. It is also an excellent record of this remarkable and historic event. His vivid description of people suggests that both Americans and Japanese have not changed basically since the middle of the nineteenth century.

The approach Perry chose in order to open Japan was to use force. It was, however, not an immediate and direct application of force. His method was to *display* American power effectively. By showing off American strength, Perry tried to let Japan herself open the country, without involving the US in the military confrontation. This was a scare tactic which succeeded. Perry's vivid description of all the details of the contacts with the Japanese reads like a drama; a well-staged show.

It is probably true to say that many of the interactions (both significant and insignificant) between people, are like dramas — great and small. In fact, Erving Goffman, a Canadian-American sociologist, suggested a sociological approach in which a certain incident is compared to a drama. There are protagonists and by-players. They perform on the stage, with a view to impressing the audience. Clothing, posture, facial movement, and other means of expression are exploited to achieve maximum effect. The performance may involve only a single person, or the collaboration of two or more people. The actors prepare their performance behind the scenes, and the audience is not allowed to see what they are actually doing there before and after the performance.

Goffman suggests that by looking at people and their behaviour from the perspective of drama, we may be able to derive a new insight into human nature. Indeed, when we read Perry's account of what he and his subordinates did in Japan, it becomes apparent that he succeeded in opening Japan precisely because he presented a very effective drama of power display. The Japanese were the audience. I would like to discuss here, therefore, how Perry planned and presented his drama. Although Goffman uses his own jargon to explain his approach, we can use simple English just as easily to set the stage and retell the story.

Perry's Performance

To begin with, we can safely assume that having made a detailed study of the literature on Japan, Perry was convinced he knew how to deal with the Japanese. In fact he stopped off at Okinawa on his way to Japan to try out his method of power display. For example, Perry consistently ignored orders from the Okinawan bureaucracy and let the crews from his squadron of four ships land and move around the island at will. Okinawan officials requested that Perry should not go to the Royal Palace, because the king's mother was ill. But this, too, was ignored, and Perry and some of his subordinates entered the palace. However, their behaviour was not rude, according to the Okinawan description of the incident. Perry offered presents to the Royal family and he also offered medicine. Perry later wrote that his approach in dealing with the Okinawans was satisfactory.

From Okinawa, Perry's squadron travelled north to the main islands of Japan. On 8 July 1853 they arrived off the town of Uraga along the Bay of Edo (Tokyo) on the main island of Honshu. The negotiations between Perry and the Japanese officials were well documented by both sides; it is worth noting that the American and Japanese descriptions are in almost complete agreement. Perry displayed power intentionally and consistently in a well calculated manner. Above all, he let the Japanese think that he was an extremely important person who was determined to achieve his goal by whatever means at his disposal.

To begin with, he refused to see Japanese officials of lower ranks. He insisted on seeing a functionary of the highest rank. Here, Perry rejected the possibility of being handled by the lower strata of Japanese bureaucracy; had he agreed to do so, it would have immediately implied that Perry was a foreigner of low status.

On 9 July, the following day, Nakajima Saburosuke, a Japanese official holding the rank of *yoriki* (police officer) wanted to see Perry but was refused. Nakajima then suggested that he might be allowed to confer with an officer of rank corresponding with his own. Perry did not allow his subordinate to answer immediately. In his own words, 'after some intentional delay,' Perry consented. A conference was then held between Nakajima and Lieutenant Contee.

Since the Dutch were the only westerners who were allowed to trade with Japan, the Dutch language was the only western language the Japanese could speak sufficiently, and the conference was held in Dutch. One of the first points Perry made through Lieutenant Contee was that he was not at all happy about having Japanese guard boats around his ships. Perry warned that if the boats were not removed immediately, he would disperse them by force. Upon receiving this threat the Japanese immediately instructed their guard boats to return to the shore, although a few stayed behind but were seen off by an armed boat from one of the American ships with a show of arms. Shortly after, the Governor's office in Uraga issued a warning in writing to all Japanese not to go near the American ships because the Americans did not like that.

On the following morning, Kayama Eizaemon, another *yoriki*, came to see Perry, but again Perry refused to see him and let Commanders Buchanan and Adams and Lieutenant Contee see Kayama because he thought Kayama held a higher position than Nakajima. Here was a very good example of Perry's careful and sensitive approach in dealing with the Japanese. When a conference was held, the Japanese officials asked many questions such as the names of the ships, the names of the officers, the total number of crew, but very few of these questions were answered and the rest were simply ignored.

The Japanese officials insisted repeatedly that the squadron must go to Nagasaki because, according to Japanese law, Nagasaki was the only place for negotiating foreign business. Perry also rejected this instruction. He stated that he purposely came to Uraga because of its proximity to Edo (present-day Tokyo) and that he had absolutely no intention of going to Nagasaki. Furthermore, he argued that the Japanese government had been notified the previous year about their planned arrival in Edo Bay. Of course, Perry was right. The fact is that, using the Dutch as intermediaries, the Americans in 1851 did notify the Japanese about their forthcoming journey to Japan, and to Edo in particular.. The document was delivered by Dutch officials to Japanese officials in Nagasaki. It was translated into Japanese but ignored by Japanese officials. As a result, the Governor's office in Uraga knew nothing about it.

Perry then threatened the Japanese officials by saying that

if the American documents could not be delivered to the Japanese government in the vicinity of his anchorage, he would go on shore with a sufficient force and make his way to Edo where he would deliver the documents — whatever the consequences of doing so might be. Kayama was also told that there was no excuse to take time to decide, and that if the Japanese were reluctant, the Americans would attack Japan and decide who would win. Perry implied that anything could happen because he was determined to achieve the objective. Here, Perry presented himself clearly as a man of power and determination.

The Japanese modified their attitudes slightly, and replied that a high official especially appointed by the Emperor would receive the documents on the shore along the Bay of Edo but an answer would be transmitted to Nagasaki through the Dutch or Chinese officials in Nagasaki. Perry again rejected this proposal. In a memorandum, he stated that he would not go to Nagasaki to receive a Japanese reply through the Dutch or Chinese or anybody. He also stated that if the letter from the American President to the Japanese Emperor was not received and duly replied to, he would consider the United States insulted and would not hold himself accountable for the consequences.

Upon receiving more threats, the Japanese yielded again. Toda Ujihide and Ido Hiromichi, the two governors of Uraga, issued an official receipt and accepted the American documents at Kurihama, located at the head of Edo Bay.

Perry's Manipulation of the Scene

In addition to the cunning presentation of himself as a person of extreme importance with a clear determination to achieve his objective, Perry skilfully manipulated the scene in order to render his performance even more effective. His subordinates cooperated well. According to Kayama, the conditions and atmosphere inside the ship suggested a state of emergency when he first conferred with three American officers. Kayama also states: 'Not only the officers but also all the aliens on board had extremely serious expressions on their faces showing that they were determined to achieve their objective...'

Perry and his squadron also attempted a large-scale manipulation of the scene. Already the day after their arrival, Perry ordered boats from the four ships to survey the Bay of Edo.

The boats were well manned and armed. Kayama told the Americans that to survey the harbour was against Japanese law. But the Americans replied that according to American law they were required to carry out a survey for the benefit of future navigation. When they were prevented from doing so by Japanese officers, the Americans produced swords and showed that they were ready to attack the Japanese officers. The Americans also fired guns into the water aiming two or three feet in front of the Japanese boat.

Later, Perry let one of his ships, the *Mississippi,* and some small boats move higher up the bay towards Edo. Perry writes: 'I had purposely sent *Mississippi* and the boats on this service, being satisfied that the very circumstance of approaching nearer to Edo with a powerful ship would alarm the authorities and induce them to give a more favourable answer to my demands...'

By such examples of power and authority, Perry and his subordinates demonstrated the *de facto* control of the Japanese territorial waters and made the stage more advantageous for themselves. The process of letting the Japanese realise that the Americans were moving around freely in the Bay of Edo and ignoring the Japanese laws had the effect of enhancing the importance and power of Perry and by implication, the importance and power of the United States.

When the Japanese finally yielded and agreed to accept the American documents, Perry's presentation was pure drama. In reading Perry's accounts, you consistently get the impression that Perry himself loved literature and theatrical works, and that he was consciously presenting himself as the protagonist. Perry writes: '...every preparation [has] been made for landing a formidable escort of officers, seamen, and marines from the respective ships. They are about 400 in number, all well armed and equipped....' Two ships of the squadron moved to a position commanding the landing place to set the stage more favourably for the Americans. The letter from President Fillmore to the Emperor and Perry's letter of credence were each contained in rosewood boxes, which were about 12 inches long, having locks, hinges, and other mountings made of solid gold. Perry records that the boxes were 'about six inches in diameter, and three deep, costing...a thousand dollars each.'

Perry's dramatisation of the event is most explicit in the following statement: 'These splendid specimens of American workmanship were covered with scarlet cloth and carried into the audience room by two of the best looking boys of the squadron, selected for the purpose, who were guarded by a couple of tall jet-black negroes, completely armed.'

The manipulation of the scene was done violently as well as ceremoniously. A Japanese officer describes the following incident: 'Sixty or seventy of them [Americans] suddenly entered the building [where the documents were to be delivered] and occupied the best corner of the room. They were all wearing a sword and a loaded...pistol. They stared at [the Japanese] and were ready to attack. Those [Japanese] in charge of the reception entrance were almost trampled over.' After this meeting, two American boats landed and tried to obtain water. Japanese officers prevented them but gave them water. The Americans produced swords and fired pistols.

Perry's manipulation of the scene did not end when the documents were handed to the Japanese. Even after this event he ordered further surveying work to be done. The purpose was clearly indicated in Perry's own records: 'To show these princes [the two governors of Uraga] how little I regarded their order for me to depart, on getting on board I immediately ordered the whole squadron underway, not to leave the bay...but to go higher up...[This] would produce a decided influence upon the pride and conceit of the government, and cause a more favourable consideration of the President's letter.' Perry continued to ignore Japanese instructions and gave the order for his squadron to anchor in an area prohibited by Japanese law.

However, Perry was not demonstrating power just for the sake of doing so. On the contrary, he was very careful in carrying out his plans. On 15 July, Perry's ship *Mississippi* was within seven miles of Edo. He then became apprehensive about alarming the Japanese too much — possibly resulting in less desirable consequences. He writes: 'Thinking that I had done enough to work up the fears of the Emperor...I caused the ship to rejoin the squadron...'

He was also sensitive enough to ensure his strategy worked. He writes: '...the nearer we approached the imperial city the more polite and friendly they became.' Perry's observation is very interesting psychoanalytically. The Japanese felt the Americans' power display intensely. The Americans were behaving freely, totally ignoring Japanese orders. The Japanese must have felt hostility and aggression towards the Americans. Yet they could not express their feelings with actions. The Americans were much stronger. The Japanese feelings became more and more intense as the Americans came closer and closer to Edo.

The defence mechanism the Japanese employed here was reaction formation. The feeling of hostility and aggression was reversed and became politeness and friendliness. This was expressed openly towards the Americans. As the Americans came closer and closer to Edo, the Japanese became more and more polite and friendly. To become more and more polite and friendly overtly meant becoming more and more covertly hostile and aggressive in Japanese minds. I think this was a culturally encouraged defence mechanism among the Japanese. Indeed, the same response in the form of smile and laughter is seen among present-day Japanese when they perceive some kind of danger. Japanese cinema quite often deals with this type of reaction.

Perry was also careful in offering or receiving presents or free supplies. After the first meeting with the American officers, Kayama offered supplies of water and refreshments, but this offer was not accepted. When *Mississippi* was within seven miles of Edo, Kayama was evidently greatly irritated and approached another ship in the squadron, the *Sasquehanna*. He begged the acceptance of a few presents, but these were once again rejected.

On 16 July, the following day, Kayama made one more attempt to offer presents. He was then told about a reciprocity of courtesy, and he agreed to receive American presents in return for the Japanese presents. In this exchange, the Americans offered articles of more value than the Japanese presents. At first, Kayama declined to accept them because he thought they were of too much value, but he finally accepted all the gifts except three swords.

On the same day in the afternoon, Kayama came on board again with a present of poultry and eggs. Perry writes regarding the present: 'Determining to be under no obligation to these people I sent in return presents of greater value to the wives of the governor and his interpreters.'

Evidently, Perry was trying to make his position advantageous over the Japanese by showing off generosity in the exchange process. To receive *more* in the exchange means the loss of power, which in turn means the recognition that the other side has more power. Furthermore, this tends to create a sense of obligation, or what Japanese call '*giri*.' In this way, Perry could undermine Kayama's power and effectiveness in the Japanese bureaucracy. In addition, Kayama's failure in the negotiations could have negative implications on the Japanese side.

3 Two Treaties and the Meiji Restoration

THE RESIDENTS of Uraga were absolutely amazed to see the American squadron. According to Iizuka Kumesaburo, a *yoriki*, they started to panic, gathering their belongings together ready to flee; the streets were chaotic. Gradually, various rumours spread through the town and gave rise to even more concern. After delivering the documents, the squadron went higher up the bay, and fired cannons. Nakane Sekko wrote in his diary: 'It sounded like a distant thunder and the mountains...echoed back the noise of the shots. This was so formidable that the people in Edo were fearful...'

When Shogun (the *de facto* head of state) Iyeyoshi was notified about the arrival of the squadron, he was greatly shocked and shaken, and was later taken ill with a high fever. The Imperial Court ordered seven temples and shrines to pray for help from the gods and Buddha in order to expel the barbarians and maintain the safety of the nation.

The American display of superior power was very effective indeed, and resulted in a Tokugawa government policy to avoid military confrontation with the Americans by not offending them. According to Gohara Sozo, another *yoriki*, the desire of the government was to handle the problem peacefully because if the Americans were offended, it would inevitably lead to grave consequences. The Japanese were told to ignore the Americans even if they should land and go to a Japanese home as long as they did not act violently. Two boats were kept near the American ships at all times to prevent anything happening that might cause the Americans to react aggresively.

At the official meeting at Kurihama where the US documents were received, the Japanese felt that the Americans ridiculed and laughed at them, but since they were instructed not to offend the Americans in any way whatsoever, they could do nothing, and they felt powerless. *Yoriki* Kayama reported that since the Japanese defence capability was clearly so inferior, they had no option but to handle the situation peacefully.

Debate in Japan

After eight days in thè Bay of Edo the American squadron left. But before leaving Perry notified the Japanese that his squadron would return to Japan in the spring of the following year in even greater strength. The *rojyu,* or the senior councillors of the Tokugawa government, solicited ideas in order to arrive at a satisfactory solution to the American demand to open the country. According to an unpublished private record, more than 800 suggestions were made and submitted. Many people also expressed their ideas without formally submitting them to the government.

Although some Japanese thought that Japan could defend herself successfully and continue to remain isolated from the rest of the world, those in the government and the influential *daimyo* (land-holding military lords) were well aware of Japan's military and technological inferiority and the consequent difficulty of maintaining the seclusion policy. Ii Naosuke, who was in charge of coastal defences along Edo Bay at the time of the Perry expedition and later became *Tairo,* a position immediately below *Shogun,* thought that because of Japan's inferior military power, it would be impossible to continue the seclusion. For this reason, he supported the principle of trade with other countries.

The influential *daimyo* Mito Naraiki was against it, even though he was quite aware of the fact that Japanese technology was inferior. Another influential *daimyo* Shimazu Nariakira was also against the opening of Japan, but he, too, knew that Japan could not fight a war successfully against a western power. Among the *kuge* (nobles), Takatsukasa Masamichi, who was *kanpaku* (Imperial regent) at the time, expressed the view that the opening of Japan could not be prevented because the *samurai* (warriors) could not successfully defend the nation.

Okudaira Masamoto, who was a less influential *daimyo*, proposed a plan to trade only with America, and if other countries should also want to trade with Japan, the Japanese could let America reject them. A similar suggestion was made by Kuroda Nagahiro, a *daimyo* with the influential background of the Shimazu family. He suggested that Japan might trade with America and Russia but not with France and England. To him, it was acceptable to fight against France and England because America and Russia would help Japan. In essence, regardless of the reasons offered, most Japanese came to accept the reality of which their government was acutely aware: that their country's military power and technology were inferior to those of the West.

The Signing of a Treaty

As promised, Perry returned to Japan the following year, with an even bigger task-force. On 11 February 1854, his squadron, this time consisting of nine ships, appeared once again in Edo Bay. Perry repeated exactly the same tactics as before. For their part, the main concern of the Japanese was not to offend the foreigners. Perry's presentation of the drama was the same, and he acted as a man of extreme importance with a clear determination to achieve his goal.

First, Perry released as little information as possible to the Japanese. His subordinates were instructed to listen to everything the Japanese had to say but to give them no unnecessary information nor to promise them anything.

Second, Perry avoided all contact with Japanese officials of lower ranks and let it be known, as before, that he would communicate only with high-ranking officials; or in his own words, 'none but the princes of the Empire.'

Third, Perry refused to meet at Kamakura, which the Japanese had officially designated as the place for the negotiations. Perry suspected what he called 'some artful design' on the part of the Japanese in choosing Kamakura. Next, the Japanese suggested Uraga, but Perry also rejected this plan on the grounds that it was unsafe and inconvenient. The Japanese kept insisting on meeting at Uraga.

Fourth, Perry implied the use of force. *Yoriki* Kayama informed the Americans that they could obtain water only at Uraga but Perry rejected this arrangement, and notified Kayama that if the Japanese did not bring water to them, he 'would send on shore and procure it by some means.'

Fifth, Perry hinted at the possibility of a war if his objectives could not be achieved. He threatened the Japanese by saying that a fleet of 100 ships could arrive in about 20 days.

The manipulation of the stage scene was also the same as in 1853. From the moment the squadron anchored, Perry ordered a survey of the harbour. In order to reject the plan to meet at Uraga, Perry also moved the squadron within eight miles of Edo. Perry writes: '...I determined to carry out my threat.'

In order not to undermine the effect of his power display, Perry was careful to negotiate supplies and exchange presents. When the Japanese officials tried to force the Americans to meet at Uraga, they offered wood and water and refreshments, but the Americans declined the offer and told the Japanese that they would not accept free supplies.

In his own words, Perry presented himself as 'a character of unreasonable obstinacy,' and as an example of power display, he succeeded. At first, the Japanese insisted that the Emperor had issued a decree which stated that the meeting had to take place at Uraga and that this was something which could not be changed. But after Perry had moved the squadron within eight miles of Edo, Kayama suddenly abandoned the ultimatum of meeting at Uraga and suggested a spot directly opposite the ships. Perry was convinced about the effectiveness of power display and proudly explained: 'I was simply adhering to a course of policy determined on after mature reflection, and which had hitherto worked so well.'

However, we might add that a good performance on stage is inextricably linked with backstage preparations which the audience are never allowed to see. According to George Henry Preble, one of Perry's subordinates, at least on 17 February, Perry was sick in bed; this was one of the factors which delayed the signing of the treaty.

At Kanagawa, where both parties agreed to meet, Perry was escorted by about 500 officers, seamen, and Marines, who were all fully armed. Twenty guns were fired in honour of the Emperor, and seventeen for the Japanese commissioners. According to Perry, this display in landing 'was made altogether for purposes of policy in accordance with the reasons already assigned,' and the reasons are 'the importance and moral influence of such show.' George Henry Preble wrote: 'The show on our side was pretty and imposing.'

Perry also displayed power concerning the content of the treaty at Kanagawa. He rejected the article in which shipwrecked men were to be sent to Nagasaki and confined there. He also rejected the article which prohibited shipwrecked American seamen from associating with the Dutch and Chinese. On these points, the Japanese yielded.

The Treaty of Peace and Amity, or the Treaty of Kanagawa, was finally signed by both parties on 31 March 1854, in the way the Americans wanted. Ido Satohiro, who actually negotiated with the Americans, wrote that they were obstinate and unjust but the Japanese were forced to yield.

According to Preble, the Japanese said that Perry had been received as an enemy but after the signing of the Treaty he was looked upon as a friend. This is a psychoanalytically suggestive statement. The Japanese were constantly threatened by the Americans and they were finally forced to sign the Treaty against their will. Furthermore, the content of the Treaty was agreed upon in the way the Americans wanted. So, how could the Japanese think of Perry as a 'friend'?

We can reasonably conclude that in this context the Japanese used reaction formation. The Japanese must have felt an intense feeling of hatred and hostility towards the Americans. Yet because of the clear superiority of the American military power, the Japanese could not express their hatred and hostility in action. But they could reverse such feelings in the form of reaction formation, which could be expressed in words and actions. Hatred and hostility became friendliness and amity. An enemy became a 'friend.' This again is a defence mechanism encouraged by Japanese culture.

Other Displays

During their second visit to Japan, the Americans demonstrated a 1/4-scale model locomotive with tender and passenger cars as well as a telegraphic system. This was an additional display of advanced western technology the sole purpose of which was to impress the Japanese. In contrast and by way of reciprocation, the Japanese organised a *sumo* wrestling demonstration. The wrestlers also carried some 200 bales of rice. An anonymous Japanese observing the scene wrote that the purpose was 'to display their strength.' One wrestler asked Perry to feel the hardness of his arms and his double bull neck. Perry writes: 'When he observed that I manifested much surprise, he exhibited his gratification by a self-satisfied grunt.'

Here, we have an interesting competition where both sides are trying to manipulate the scene. Both the Americans and the Japanese are on stage, and at the same time, they are also audiences. In this situation, those who present a more effective show can control the scene and become the actors; the other side is changed into the audience.

It appears that the Americans presented a more effective show in this competition and won the game. Upon seeing the western inventions, the Japanese were amazed, excited, astonished, and delighted. But in contrast, Perry was not impressed by the Japanese show. He thought *sumo* 'seemed to be very foolish' and the wrestlers made a noise 'similar to that of dogs in combat.' Preble also wrote: 'At first, the exhibition was interesting but it soon grew tedious from repetition.'

However, in addition, the Japanese had an entirely different form of display to offer the Americans. Preble describes what he saw when he and other crew members surveyed the Bay of Edo. He writes: 'The inhabitants crowded the hill, and beckoned us on shore, and by the most unmistakable signs invited our intercourse with their women. One female went so far as to raise her drapery and expose her person to us.'[1] In addition to Perry himself, at least three of his crew members, George Henry Preble, S. Wells Williams, and Francis L. Hawks, kept detailed diaries during their visit to Japan, each of which is full of interesting descriptions of this nature.

Consul General Harris and the Signing of Another Treaty

The Americans consistently demonstrated to the Japanese how inferior their military and technology were; it is no surprise to discover therefore, that in 1853, immediately after Perry's first visit, the government removed the ban on the building of large ships. Until then, because of the Tokugawa seclusion policy, it was against the law to build ships big enough to sail abroad. However, the government was quick to realise the importance of building a navy.

The government continued the same policy of developing the military after the signing of the treaty. When the price of iron and copper went up, the government even tried to use temple bells for making cannons; this plan failed following protests by the priests. A naval academy started instruction in 1855 in which Dutch naval officers were employed as instructors using a Dutch ship. A year later, an academy for the army was opened.

As a result of the Treaty of Peace and Amity, Townsend Harris was appointed as the first American Consul General at Shimoda. He used the same tactics of power display as Perry did. In 1857 at a conference with Hotta Masayoshi, who was the Minister of Foreign Affairs, Harris emphasised the advancement of western technology in recent years and the danger of England as a colonising power. At the same time, Harris stated that Japan would not be invaded by a foreign power if there were another treaty with the United States.

When the Japanese were indecisive regarding the signing of another treaty with the United States, Harris decided on scare tactics. Or in his own words, he says: 'I determined to bring about a crisis....' Harris threatened one of the two governors of Shimoda, Inouye Kiyonao, with the dispatch of a US naval fleet to Japan. The threat was effective. In Harris's own words, '[p]oor Shinano [Governor of Shimoda] listened in evident trepidation....' Here, the governor failed to control his emotion and inadvertently revealed his fear. He lost the game.

Harris was quite satisfied with the result. He writes: '...by taking a bold attitude and assuming a threatening tone, I should at once bring them to terms.' Indeed, a week later, the Japanese yielded to all the demands Harris had made, and they agreed to begin free trade with America, to allow America to station a minister in Edo, and to open another port instead of Shimoda. Harris noted that the Governor smiled more after the threat. Here again is the Japanese smile resulting from a reaction formation due to threat and hatred.

The Tokugawa government tried to obtain an imperial rescript in order to sign the commercial treaty, but Emperor

Komei had no desire to issue such a rescript. On 14 June 1858, having realised what was happening on the Japanese side, Harris once again reverted to threat. He notified the Tokugawa government that unless the commercial treaty was signed forthwith a French-British squadron would arrive in Edo Bay within weeks and that the Japanese would have to suffer the consequences. The government had no choice but to sign the treaty without an imperial rescript.

Anti-Foreign Reactions and the Meiji Restoration

Since most of the opinions expressed in response to Perry's demand to open Japan were against it, it is understandable that after the signing of the two treaties, anti-foreign feelings among some Japanese were expressed openly and sometimes violently. In 1861, Ohashi Totsuan wrote: '...by obtaining an imperial rescript to kill and expel barbaric aliens, let patriots throughout Japan sweep away the stinkers with repugnant odour.' In 1862, Kusaka Genzui urged people to start attacking and expelling the 'burglars' at once. Otherwise, he thought, Japan would inevitably end up as a colony.

Anti-foreign feelings were expressed not only in writing, but also in action. Between 1859 and 1864, Russian, British, Dutch, Chinese, and American subjects were attacked and sometimes killed (on at least eight occasions). Even Japanese employed by foreign diplomatic legations were killed. Terrorism was also directed against Japanese who supported the opening of Japan. The Minister of Foreign Affairs warned all diplomatic agents in Edo that 500 *ronin*, or warriors without a lord, were planning attacks against diplomatic legations. Foreign residents in Japan recognised that the level of terrorism directed at them generally corresponded with the presence of foreign warships in the waters near Edo.

When British subjects were attacked by *samurai* of the Satsuma clan at Namamugi near Yokohama in 1862, one man, Richardson, was killed and two men and a woman were wounded. As a result of this incident, the British despatched seven ships the following year to Kagoshima, which was a major city of the Satsuma clan. A war started and Kagoshima was burned, and some of the batteries were dismantled. The Satsuma clan was forced to accept the fact that they were not strong enough to fight the westerners.

In 1863, the Choshu clan, which had adopted the most extreme anti-foreign attitude, began to attack western ships which passed through the straight of Shimonoseki. As a result, a fleet consisting of 17 English, American, French, and Dutch ships attacked the Shimonoseki batteries in 1864 and temporarily occupied the area. This defeat forced the Japanese to accept their military and technological inferiority and the impossibility of expelling foreigners from Japan by force.

For example, in 1864, after the conflict, Godai Saisuke of the Satsuma clan, who was taken by the British as a prisoner-of-war, submitted a suggestion to his clan. The document stated: 'The five continents are in a state of chaos. If a [weak] country agrees to have a treaty, a strong country wants to trade. If such a demand is rejected, the strong country attacks and engulfs it. This is the general principle on earth and we can do nothing to change it...'

In view of the increasing turmoil in Japan, Shogun Yoshinobu issued a statement in 1867 in which he recognised the difficulty of ruling the country and a need for a change. He stated that by transferring the ruling of Japan to the Emperor, Japan could become competitive with other countries. Emperor Meiji responded with comments concerning the grave nature of the crisis facing Japan — worse than anything since the first Perry incident — and in doing so accepted the transfer of power. This resulted in what has been called the Meiji Restoration of 1868.

4 Processes of Westernisation

BECAUSE THE military and technological inferiority of Japan had been fully appraised following the appearance of Commodore Perry's squadron in 1852 and 1853, but particularly and most decisively after the two conflicts with foreign powers in 1863 and 1864, the Japanese began to express the need for introducing western technology and science in order to deal with the western threat. Indeed, despite the seclusion policy which had been in force for over 200 years, there were many well informed Japanese scholars who were quite aware of the latest innovations in the West.

For example, in 1858 a private scholar Sakuma Zozan wrote: '...ever since Columbus discovered the New World, Copernicus advanced the heliocentric theory, Newton discovered the Law of Gravity, and after the three great inventions, all sciences have been solidly established... Because of [these achievements] Europe and America gradually changed... and are now in an amazing and formidable condition. [The only way for the Japanese to deal with the difficulty] is to imitate good things which the enemy has.' I think ultimately, this intense awareness of introducing and imitating western science and technology paved the way for a series of psychoanalytic responses and, consequently, the westernisation of Japan.

The Need of Western Technology as a Source of Psychological Stress

Before and after the Meiji Restoration of 1868, the Japanese actively expressed their social and political ideas by means of mottoes. Interestingly enough, they almost always used four Chinese characters. This was an effective way to convey a certain point of view and thereby to encourage people to think and act and change Japan along certain lines.

Immediately after the Perry incident, two mottoes were actively used in Japan. One was '*sonno jyoi*' (worship the Emperor, expel the barbarians), and the other was '*fukoku kyohei*' (enrich the country, strengthen the military). The meaning is quite clear in both mottoes. The Japanese feared and hated the Americans, and at the same time, they were intensely aware of the weakness of their military power.

Godai Saisuke wrote in 1864 that western countries had achieved *fukoku kyohei* successfully and were dominating the world as a result. He stated that the damage the Satsuma clan suffered in the war was a godsend in that the incident taught some stupid Japanese a lesson. By achieving *fukoku kyohei*, revenge was possible, he said.

Sakuma Zozan also expressed the same idea in 1862, although he did not use the expression *fukoku kyohei*. He thought that the development of arts, sciences, and technology in the world was a fate determined by Heaven, and that seclusion of a country was possible only when enough national strength and technology were present. Through contact with outside barbarians, the Japanese could acquire the advanced aspects of other countries. Then Japan could overtake other countries and so prevent a foreign power from attacking or invading Japan.

Here the ideology of *fukoku kyohei* is to acquire western science and technology in order to fight against the western threat, and this is likely to have created a psychological conflict in the minds of the Japanese. On the one hand, the Japanese feared and hated the western powers, and this was expressed by the motto, *sonno jyoi*. For the nation as a whole, the opinion was predominantly against yielding to Perry's demand to open the country. Even Sakuma Zozan, who insisted on the policy of *fukoku kyohei* hated the West intensely. Nevertheless, against her will as a nation, Japan was forced to open the country by yielding to the Americans' power display.

Fukuzawa Yukichi, one of Japan's leading intellectuals, who personally witnessed and experienced the turmoil of the period, wrote that, in their hearts, even those in the Tokugawa government who actually carried out the work of opening up Japan disliked foreigners intensely and some even hated them. Indeed, Abe Masahiro, who was the key person in the Perry negotiations, wrote: '... who would handle a situation like this happily? I could not stop shedding bloody tears. This is indeed repugnant and painful.' The fact that terrorist acts against foreigners began so soon after the signing of the two treaties suggests the intensity of such feelings among the Japanese generally.

As individual human beings, westerners were often considered ugly and similar to beasts. In 1807, a scholar wrote that westerners were actually beasts although they looked similar to human beings. They were also called 'dog-sheep.' Even after the Japanese came to realise that their technology was inferior, some continued to believe that western physical characteristics were unattractive. For example, Muragaki Norimasa, who went to Washington D.C. in 1860 as a member of the Japanese mission to exchange treaty ratifications, wrote that American women were unattractive because their hair was red and their eyes were similar to those of dogs.

But despite the presence of such feelings, the Japanese were forced to come to terms with the inescapable fact that to survive (and succeed) in the new world order they had to become like westerners by imitating their technology and military. Even Yoshida Shoin, who showed an extreme xenophobic attitude, tried to leave for America illegally with Perry's squadron in order to see the world.

There was really no choice. It was impossible to continue the seclusion policy because the western powers would not allow Japan to do so; by the same token, Japanese military inferiority eliminated the option of expelling the 'invaders.' This option would only become available if Japan acquired western knowledge and skills and western military know-how and technology. By definition, therefore, the Japanese were placed in a state of psychological stress against their will: they hated the westerners yet they had to become like them, and here was the source of the stress.

Rationalisation

In order to deal with this problem, there developed two forms of psychoanalytic responses (defence mechanisms) in the minds of the Japanese. These were: (1) rationalisation; and (2) identification with the aggressor.

The Japanese began to use the expression, 'wakon yosai' (Japanese spirit, western skill). By this, they meant that a combination of the traditional Japanese mentality and the advanced western technology was the best solution to the problem they were faced with. Already in 1854, Sakuma Zozan wrote: 'To study and master both Eastern morality and Western technology... and then to give society their benefits and to contribute to the nation is one of the five pleasures.'

Another scholar, Hashimoto Sanai, wrote that westerners were superior in technology, but Japanese were superior to westerners in ethics and morality. He was implying that both westerners and Japanese were advanced in two different aspects. For both scholars, but especially for Sakuma Zozan, the implication was that the Japanese could remain as they always had been in mentality, but by accepting western technology, they could become even better.

Such thinking could be considered a form of rationalisation. Since there was no choice but to accept western technology and to become westernised technologically, the Japanese now had to explain *what* they were going to do and *how* they were going to do it. The answer was to use the motto, *wakon yosai*. This concept enabled the Japanese to convince themselves that to accept western technology was a way of becoming an even better people, and that what they were accepting was only western technology, not their mentality. It was a way of reassuring themselves that they were merely borrowing western technology but that at heart they would always remain Japanese. The logic of *wakon yosai*, therefore, enabled the Japanese to cope with the repugnant idea of becoming like westerners whom they hated.

I should add that the Japanese had already used the same logic in earlier times. Before the rise of the motto, *wakon yosai*, there was already another motto, 'wakon kansai' (Japanese spirit, Chinese skill). Evidently, the Japanese were faced with a similar problem when they accepted so much from Chinese culture centuries earlier, and they tried to deal with the problem by insisting on *wakon kansai*. The logic of *wakon kansai* no doubt facilitated the use of the new motto, *wakon yosai*.

Initial Phase of Identification

Another defence mechanism the Japanese used was identification with westerners as the aggressor. The Japanese tried to deal with the western threat by identifying with westerners. There are at least five reasons why this defence mechanism was triggered in the minds of the Japanese — both before and after the Meiji Restoration.

First, when the Japanese were already faced with Perry's demand, they casually showed responses which suggest that they were unintentionally identifying with the westerners. That is, the Japanese imagined they were placing themselves in the position of the most threatening people at the time.

For example, *daimyo* Okudaira Masamoto proposed that Japan should let America expel other foreign powers in return for Japan's agreement to trade with America. Quite clearly, Okudaira took it for granted that the Americans were the most powerful people among the westerners, and believing that there were enemies amongst the western nations, he imagined that America would expel all the other foreign powers. In this way, through the eyes of the Americans, he thought he could expel Japan's enemies.

Another *daimyo*, Kuroda Nagahiro, thought that America and Russia would help Japan fight against France and England if Japan would agree to trade with them. At the time the Russians were almost as threatening as the Americans to the Japanese, and he was identifying with the two most threatening peoples. Furthermore, by identifying with the Americans and the Russians, he looked on them as two helpful and friendly nations. At least to him, America and Russia no longer existed as threatening nations as a result of identification.

Another example involved a Dutch officer. In October 1853, immediately after Japan's first contact with Perry, the governor's office in Nagasaki asked a Dutch naval officer stationed in Nagasaki how Japan might handle the problem of increasing numbers of foreign ships coming to Japan. They asked the Dutch officer to state his opinion 'by assuming to be a Japanese,' (if translated literally). This incident suggests that when the Japanese were uncertain as to a proper course of action to take, they began to identify with the westerners and also as a result, asked them to identify with the Japanese in order to obtain greater insight.

Casual psychological responses of this nature could easily lead to more extensive and intentional identification with the westerners, because they were consistently threatening the Japanese. Furthermore, the threat was becoming more and more intense. Indeed, at a shipboard banquet after the signing of the Treaty in 1854, the chief Japanese commissioner's secretary threw his arms about Perry's neck in his drunken embrace and repeated in Japanese: 'Japan and America, all the same heart.'

Psychologists and psychoanalysts tell us that we inadvertently reveal ourselves when we are under intoxication or hypnosis. I think it is very difficult to look upon people who *force* you to do something against your will as 'friends.' Besides, the consequence of the action is extremely serious and there is no alternative. You are told you must do it, and you do it. After that, you are likely to intensify your hatred even further. But you cannot express hatred or release aggression. These emotions are too strong. So you resort to some form of defence mechanism. In the case of this drunken secretary, he was unable to express his identification with the Americans when he was sober. That was too repugnant. He could only do that when intoxicated.

.   .   .

Second, there are known cases in which extremely xenophobic Japanese changed their minds after their trip to Europe or America. For example, Ikeda Naganobu went to France in 1863 as the head of a Japanese diplomatic delegation, and by being exposed to French civilisation, he changed his xenophobic attitude and began to advocate the policy of opening Japan. Two Japanese, Ito Harusuke and Inouye Monta, were once active haters of foreigners and they participated in the burning-down of the British Consulate in Edo in 1862. But after their stay in England as students, they became active supporters of the opening of Japan.

In these examples, it is conceivable that by actually being in a western country, a xenophobic Japanese was overwhelmed by the reality of western strength and power, and in order to deal with the threat at first hand, identification with the aggressor was inevitable. As a result, such Japanese began to talk like westerners and insisted on the opening of Japan. Identification with the aggressor took place only after being exposed to the reality of the West, because the threat of the West was much more intense when a Japanese was actually in a western country. To maintain the same xenophobic attitude was no longer possible or effective under these circumstances.

. . .

Third, expressions gradually emerged which neatly summarise the psychology of identification with the West as the aggressor. The motto '*datsua nyuo*' (leave Asia, join Europe) began to be used sometime after the Meiji Restoration, and this unmistakably urges the Japanese in a certain direction. Through this motto, the Japanese were told that Japan should not remain as an Asian country; instead, Japan should become like a European country. Under this motto, the new Meiji government officially and actively advanced the westernisation policy. The purpose was very specific and the type of military they wanted was also very specific — not just some sort of 'western' military. The government decided that the Japanese navy should be like the British navy, and the Japanese army should be like the French army.

Another motto '*bunmei kaika*' (being civilised) first appeared in print in 1868. This motto urged the Japanese to accept western civilisation; often uncritically. In many cases, anything western was imitated and accepted as something good and up to date. One aspect of *bunmei kaika* was to change the old ideas regarding racial differences. The Japanese were informed that human beings as well as birds, beasts, and plants, differ because of the climatic and environmental differences, and that this is a universal and natural law. Possibly, this motto was instrumental in assisting Japanese change their traditional attitude towards westerners who were perceived as 'beasts' and in facilitating identification with them.

Acceptance of Western Ideology

Fourth, as a result of *bunmei kaika*, the Japanese began to accept even the non-technological, non-material aspects of western civilisation. When Japan was forced to sign the treaties with

America in 1854 and 1858, the Japanese felt only the inferiority of their technology and military power, and they felt the need to acquire only the technology of the West. This attitude was most clearly summarised by the motto, *wakon yosai*. In essence, what the Japanese tried to convince themselves of was that, although western technology was necessary for them in order to survive, this was all they had to acquire, because they perceived themselves to be superior to westerners in spirit and thus there was no need to acquire the ideological aspects of the West.

But as time went on, it soon became impossible to maintain this position. Already in 1879, Yoshioka Noriaki wrote: 'There are two ways of being civilised. One is to be civilised in mentality, and the other is to be civilised in material objects. To be civilised mentally is the foundation and material civilisation is based on it.' Among the ideas which began to be introduced to the Japanese (or in the case of Christianity reintroduced) were freedom and civil rights.

For example, in 1886, Ozaki Hiromichi wrote that the great revolution in Japan was to take place not only in politics, but also in society in general, customs, practices, religion, skills, arts, as well as in everyday thinking. Among these, the changes in politics and religion were most important to him. In his opinion, both Confucianism and Buddhism could not be the source of morality. By introducing Christianity, he thought, the foundation of Japanese civilisation could be established for the first time because the introduction of machines, customs, and practices without Christianity was incomplete. Tsuda Masamichi suggested in 1874 that the government should employ westerners to teach Christianity to the Japanese because Christianity was the religion of civilised people. Therefore, he argued, it was entirely logical for the Japanese to be exposed to Christianity.

In 1871, an anonymous article entitled 'In the Style of a Document From a Westerner to the Emperor' was published in a Japanese magazine, in which the author suggested that the Emperor should be baptised and become the head of a church. If he takes this course of action, the article said, the kings of the western countries would respect and congratulate the Emperor because Japan is the Europe in the Orient. It later turned out that this article had actually been written by a Japanese thinker, Nakamura Masanao.

This incident is most interesting in three ways. First, the

author reflects the attitudes of some intellectuals in Japan immediately after the Meiji Restoration who believed in the necessity of becoming Christians in order to be civilised. Second, the fact that the author pretended to be a westerner suggests identification. Third, by writing an article pretending to be a westerner, he probably believed that it would be more effective in influencing the Japanese. If such thinking was present in his mind, the reason could be traced back to Japan's continuous exposure to the 'western' factor from the time of the arrival of Perry, namely, the power of westerners to achieve and realise an objective. This view, of course, is the result of identification with the aggressor.

The ideas of freedom and civil rights also began to be discussed by Japanese intellectuals immediately after the Meiji Restoration. For example, in 1875, Kato Hiroyuki thought that the lack of civil rights was an indication of not being civilised. Oi Kentaro wrote in 1890 that education, religion, and Confucianism were not sufficient to reform society. By spreading the ideology of freedom and equality, social thought could be reformed.

The emphasis on the importance of these non-technological aspects of western civilisation is most important in understanding the change within Japanese society and must be fully recognised. As mentioned above, immediately after the arrival of Perry, the Japanese felt the need to acquire only western technology in order to fight back: because, they thought, the Japanese were superior to the westerners in non-technological aspects, there was no need to acquire western thoughts as well, including Christianity. However, less than 30 years later, the Japanese were discussing the need of acquiring these aspects of western civilisation which, according to some Japanese, were even more important than the technological aspects.

Japan as a 'Western' Nation

Fifth, still later, the Japanese clearly began to consider Japan as a 'western' nation. For example, in 1882, Fukuzawa Yukichi, one of the most influential thinkers of the period, wrote a newspaper editorial entitled 'Oppression can be pleasant.' In this editorial, he mentions the arrogance of the British in Hong Kong and he states that he does not feel sorry for the Chinese nor does he hate the British. He 'entirely envied the British and admired their oppression' when he was in Hong Kong. He thinks that their exercise of power is even stronger than that of the Tokugawa officers in the past, and that this must create a wonderful feeling.

Fukuzawa goes on to say that by increasing international trade, the Japanese Empire can acquire a large naval force and enhance Japanese prestige. After that, the Japanese can control the Chinese even more effectively than the British can. Even the British can be handled like slaves. He closes the editorial as follows: 'The reason why we are unhappy about foreigners now is because we still cannot escape their domination. My desire is that we should dominate their domination, and that only we dominate the whole world. This is my only desire.'

In 1885, Fukuzawa also wrote that by learning the method of western civilisation, Japan must reject the neighbouring backward countries such as China and Korea. This view of Japan as a 'western' nation became increasingly clear during and after the wars with China and Russia. Shortly after, Japan began developing her own colonial empire by imitating the colonialism of the western countries. But the West rejected Japan precisely because of this. I shall elaborate on this aspect in the next two chapters.

In conclusion, therefore, we can say that identification with westerners as the aggressor gradually took place in the minds of the Japanese over a period of time. But already by the early 1880s, as we have seen, the process of identification was almost complete. From then on, the history of Japan consistently shows the phenomena of identification with the West.

5 Unsuccessful Identification

THE WESTERNISATION OF Japan was far more extensive than the Japanese themselves could have imagined possible. It is certainly a fact, however, that when the Japanese reformers were planning the introduction of western technology in order to fight back and challenge western domination, the picture of Japan only a few decades later was totally unforeseeable. Some of the principal issues and preoccupations before and after the turn of the century were of major importance, while others as we look at them from today's vantage point, were incredible or amusing.

For example, there was the problem of the unequal treaties with the western nations which Japan was forced to sign. The Japanese wanted to abolish these treaties, and for this purpose, the Japanese government financed the building of the *Rokumeikan* which opened in 1883. The *Rokumeikan* was a social club in Tokyo where upper class Japanese men and women could emulate western culture and dress and enjoy conversation, dance and music. The Japanese reasoned that, before equal treaties could be considered, westerners must be able to live among the Japanese without danger. Therefore, they further reasoned, Japan must offer similar western social environments. This meant western clothes, western social relations, western dances, and western parties. It was a conscious effort to become westernised, but it is also possible to argue that because of the identification factor, such activities could be carried out.

Others were not eager to have westerners living among the

Japanese. I should add straight away, however, that this was not a desire to segregate the 'barbarians.' By the 1880s westerners were no longer considered 'barbarians.' On the contrary, under the influence of the philosophy of evolution, Japanese intellectuals such as Fukuzawa Yukichi began to think of westerners as 'civilised,' whereas the Japanese, still in the earlier stage of development, were the 'barbarians.'

Precisely because of this new way of thinking, some Japanese did not want to have westerners living amongst them. One reason was that the westerners might manipulate Japanese politics or the economy, because they were thought to be more advanced than the Japanese. Another reason mentioned was that if a superior people, namely the westerners, should live with an inferior people, namely the Japanese, the inferior people would decrease in population and decline.

Indeed, some Japanese believed that they were biologically inferior to westerners and suggested various measures for improvement. For example, in his book published in 1884 Takahashi Yoshio, a student of the influential thinker, Fukuzawa Yukichi, proposed that by means of intermarriage with westerners (applying the principle of breeding goldfish!), the Japanese race could be improved biologically. Interbreeding is beneficial to an inferior race, and he argued, since the Japanese are inferior to westerners biologically, the Japanese will gain by intermarriage. On this ground, he advocated intermarriage with westerners.

The same point of view was advanced by Mori Arinori, who was the first Minister of Education in the new Meiji government. He told Japanese students studying in the United States to marry American women and return home with them in order to improve the Japanese race. Naturally, there were strong reactions in Japan against such a view. For example, Kato Hiroyuki wrote sarcastically that, in order to solve the problem, it would be easier for the Japanese to leave Japan or to commit suicide collectively and give away the land to the westerners.

The Notion of East *versus* West

In addition to identification, another response to the western threat was the notion of common interest. According to this approach, the crisis caused by the western threat should not be seen as an isolated problem for Japan, but as a crisis for Asia as a whole. The western threat, therefore, could be dealt with more successfully from this perspective.

This idea seems to have developed originally in response to the outcome of the first Opium War between China and England. For example, in 1808, Sato Nobuhiro expressed a strong fear of China as a military power. But, forty years later, after seeing China's miserable defeat, he no longer saw China as a threat: the West was the new danger. In 1849, he proposed cooperation with China, so that China [literally] could be the 'defence wall to the western side of Japan [against the West].'

Other thinkers were not so explicit in emphasising the advantage for the survival of Japan, but the objective was very much the same. Already in 1825, Aizawa Yasushi wrote that only China and Japan were not contaminated by Christianity or Islam, and that China and Japan must cooperate in order to prevent European expansionism. In the case of another thinker, Sugita Junzan, the problem was a racial one. According to him, the peoples of the yellow race were being conquered, subjugated, and humiliated by the white race. The solution, as he saw it, was to unite the peoples of Asia against the whites. Thus, by changing the political climate of Asia as a whole, Japan could also develop, he thought.

It is interesting to note here, by the way, that the Japanese always described the lighter shades of their skin as white, and they never considered that they were 'yellow.' Therefore, by classifying the Japanese as 'yellow,' he was accepting the western evaluation and classification in this geographic context, despite his anti-western attitude.

In 1885, a group of Japanese activists led by Oi Kentaro were arrested in Osaka for trying to assist activists in Korea by supplying them with weapons. They had taken the view that the Koreans and the Japanese were brothers and they thought they could provide security and happiness to the Koreans by helping to instigate reform. They believed in the necessity of improving conditions in Asia, and for this reason, they wanted to collaborate with reformers in Japan, Korea, and China. The completion of the Trans-Siberian Railway was seen as the beginning of turmoil in the East in which the future survival of Japan was at stake.

Another political thinker, Tarui Tokichi, argued in 1893 that Japan and Korea should unite and build a new country which was to be called 'Daito,' meaning "The Great East.' He thought it was a disadvantage for both countries to remain as two separate states. Only by uniting could both Japan and Korea develop.

He stated that although Korea was poor, its territory was half as large as Japan, and after unification, she could become more prosperous. In the past, the Japanese had learned from the Koreans, and to teach them in turn would be an expression of gratitude to them. If Korea were invaded, even without unification, Japan would still be exposed to a danger. But since the Koreans were big and strong, by teaching them the Japanese method of fighting and by supplying them with Japanese weapons, they would be able to do enough to prevent a Russian invasion. Thus, in Tarui's opinion, the advantages for Korea would also benefit Japan.

Tarui also saw the problem in racial terms. He argued that the peoples of the same race in Asia must unite and compete against the other races. Therefore, it was also desirable to unite with China, but the conditions in China were not favourable for unification, and for the time being, therefore, 'Daito' and China would have to work together through an alliance. The responsibility of Japan and China in Asia was great, because without these two countries, the white race would enslave the yellow race exactly as they had enslaved the Africans. The western desire for the conquest and genocide of the yellow race was clear, and if the yellow race did not fight back and win the competition, the white race would engulf them. The only way to do this was to unite and to develop the power and strength of a single unified Asian race, he said.

The Rise of Japanese Expansionism as a Result of Identification

Identification with the West and the development of the military logically lead to expansionism and colonialism, which were seen as the hallmarks of success and the dominant characteristics among the great European trading nations. Indeed, this is exactly the view the Japanese took and acted accordingly. Already, this idea had been mooted as early as 1798 in a book by Honda Toshiaki. A century later, after the beginning of the extensive westernisation of Japan, Takegoshi Yosaburo, a historian, published a book on China in 1894. In a chapter entitled 'We cannot give a civilisation to China without using the military,' he stated: 'I have a great calling to promote a civilisation to the east. And if I want to promote a civilisation to the east, first of all I must promote a civilisation to China.' In 1899, Takayama Chogyu, an influential journalist, wrote unmistakably: 'we admire Anglo-Saxon imperialism and we hope our imperialism does not differ from theirs.'

When the Japanese realised that they had already acquired enough western science and technology as symbolised by the military, they began to think about using their power by imitating the West. In 1873, the Japanese cabinet seriously discussed the possibility of invading Korea as a means of dealing with the frustration of the unsuccessful *samurai* in the new era, because there was no place for them in Japanese society after the Meiji Restoration. The only excuse for planning such an invasion was that Korea accused Japan of westernisation by yielding to the pressures from the West.

The leading protagonist of this plot was Saigo Takamori who stated that the objective was 'to enhance Japan by transferring a desire to start a civil war in Japan to another country [Korea].' He failed to mobilise opinion, and he was forced to start a civil war in Japan instead. He failed here, too, and finally committed suicide. Although Japan did not invade Korea in 1873, the fact that the cabinet considered the issue seriously suggests that the plan itself was not completely ruled out by the Japanese government. Indeed, the same government planned to invade Taiwan the following year. Furthermore, by claiming that a Japanese ship of war was attacked by Korean forces, Japan threatened Korea and forced her to sign a treaty to open the country in 1876. This, of course, was an almost exact reproduction of what the Americans did to the Japanese just over twenty years earlier. But the Japanese went further in colonising Korea. In 1905 Japan began to control Korea officially, and in 1910 Korea was fully annexed to Japan.

From the Korean point of view, Saigo Takamori was a very offensive man because of his schemes to invade Korea. On the other hand, to the Japanese he was a tragic hero, who was unable to achieve his plan and was finally forced to commit suicide. Indeed, a bronze statue of Saigo Takamori now stands in Ueno Park, Tokyo, and is a recognised tourist attraction!

Psychoanalytically, there are both projection and displacement characteristics in these incidents. The Japanese were unable to express their hostility and aggression directly towards a western nation, at least at the time, because their military capability was inadequate. However, the Japanese already knew that they were stronger than the Koreans. So, by picking on the Koreans quickly with some spurious excuse that they were being 'unfriendly,' projection was possible. The Japanese government argued: 'Korea is hostile and they want to attack us.' By looking at Korea this way, Japan also could release her hostility and aggression onto Korea, instead of a western nation. This was of course displacement.

The gradual development of Japanese arrogance towards other Asian countries began to be expressed more and more openly. Even those Japanese, such as Sugita Junzan, who used to talk about cooperation in Asia changed their minds, and they began instead to despise the other Asian nations and to propose invasion of these countries. After seeing both China and Europe, Sugita wrote in 1886 that to cooperate with China and to assist her would mean a disaster to both Japan and China, and that in such a case Japan would not be able to remain independent of the western colonial powers. His conclusion was that instead of resisting western colonial power by cooperating with the other Asian nations, it would be more advantageous for Japan to become a colonial power herself and join the West in colonising Asia. Here is a clear change in his perspective. He now advocates colonialism as a result of identification with the West. This change took place after the expansion and modernisation of the Japanese military forces.

A magazine called *Kokumin no Tomo* (Friends of the People) was eager to advocate Japanese colonialism quite explicitly. In 1894, immediately before the outbreak of the Sino-Japanese War, the magazine argued that the nation posing the biggest threat to Japan was China and not one of the European powers. The anonymous author of the article stated that basically the Chinese had an 'invading mentality' and that consequently the neighbouring countries were actually under threat. Since Japan, however, was about to establish itself as a great country, China and Japan would end up in a state of 'to kill, or be killed.' The 'Great Japan' would be brought about by Japanese expansionism, but the Chinese were likely to be in those regions of the world which the Japanese wished to colonise. If the Chinese were allowed to do as they please, therefore, there would be no territory available to build the 'Great Japan.' Thus, a confrontation with China was racially and nationally inevitable and logical. It was quite simply a matter of life or death.

At the time, this was not a particularly extreme view as a political ideology. In 1895, Mutsu Munemitsu, who was responsible for the Japanese diplomatic activities in connection with the Sino-Japanese War thought that this war was essentially the result of a collision between the old eastern civilisation and the new western civilisation, indicating his understanding of Japan as a 'western' power. Even Uchimura Kanzo, who was considered a leading Christian thinker in Japan at that time, considered Japan as a 'small country representing the new civilisation' and China as a 'large country representing the old civilisation' and claimed that a war between such countries was justifiable. In fairness to him, I should add that he later regretted taking such a position, and spoke out against the Russo-Japanese War.

Nevertheless, generally speaking, as a result of identification with the West these political ideas which were being expressed immediately before the turn of the century clearly show that Japan was increasingly seen by the Japanese themselves as a 'western' colonising power. A desire to cooperate with the other Asian countries is no longer present; furthermore, it is now seen as natural and logical for Japan to colonise them.

After winning the Sino-Japanese War in 1895, the ideology of Japanese expansionism began to appear even more clearly and openly. Several influential journals advocated the political and economic expansion of Japan. In the first issue of the new journal *Toyo Keizai Shimpo* (Eastern Economic News) the editorial advanced the view that the future of Japan was to export finished products to the underdeveloped countries, and that if Japan did not control trade in the East soon, Japan would never be able to do so in the future. The purpose of starting a new journal was to inform Japanese businessmen about the economic conditions of the world, especially in the East.

Another journal, *Chuo Koron* (Central Review) was launched in 1899, and in its first editorial it was stated that, as a reaction to the earlier conservatism of international isolation and xenophobia, they were advocating a much bolder approach to westernisation and international relations. If Japan wanted to develop further, even more westernisation was necessary. Westernisation was, in their opinion, the ideology of the world, and by means of this ideology, the world could be unified.

Yet another journal, *Taiyo* (The Sun) expressed a similar view regarding Japanese expansion into the world. The idea of expansionism in these publications was not especially anti-western. In fact, *Chuo Koron* supported expansionism by fully accepting westernisation. The first issue's editorial was implying that, since the western way of thinking was valid for the whole world, Japan should be able to develop further by becoming even more westernised and by accepting the ideology of the West, including expansionism.

In 1902, Japan and Great Britain became allies through the signing of the Anglo-Japanese Alliance, and many Japanese were truly delighted. For example, in the editorial of 14 February, 1902, the *Jiji Shimpo*, an important daily newspaper of the time, wrote: 'Only a little more than 40 years after the opening of the country, and only five or six years after displaying the true power of our country by defeating China, we have enhanced the status of our country this much. We have truly become one of the most powerful countries in the world. We are astonished. We feel we are dreaming. Is this a dream? No, this is certainly not a dream.'

Two years later, immediately before the Russo-Japanese War, the same newspaper published another editorial on 2 February, 1904. The writer stated: 'I am very anxious to reproduce the battles of Trafalgar and Waterloo in the lands and waters of the Far East, so that Japan can truly become the Great Britain of the East.'

After the outbreak of war with Russia on 14 February, 1904, the *Jiji Shimpo* again published another interesting editorial entitled 'American Goodwill.' It said: 'Our relationship with the United States is quite different from the relationship with any other nation. To begin with, they urged us to open the country some 40 years ago. Since then, the United States guided us in a variety of ways in order to let Japan join the group of the advanced, civilised countries. We can never forget their goodwill...Although Japan is a bit behind, we are following the road to civilisation boldly and confidently under the direction of Great Britain and the United States.' Here, the author of the editorial is advocating war against Russia because that is what an advanced western country is supposed to do, and Japan has more or less become one such country thanks to Great Britain and the United States.

Realisation of the Unsuccessful Identification

According to the psychoanalytical concept of the Oedipus conflict (see p. 141), a little boy loves his mother but realises his father also exists as a rival. Here, the boy usually solves this conflict by identifying with the father. By placing himself in his father's position through his imagination and understanding, the boy can love his mother through the eyes of the father, and at the same time, he is loved by his father because he is similar to him. Identification with the father as the aggressor can bring about these less dangerous results.

Generally speaking, to identify with the aggressor in a situation like this produces two positive results: (1) to reduce and possibly eliminate the fear and anxiety of being exposed to the aggressor, because a person now thinks and feels precisely as the aggressor does; and (2) to please the aggressor by becoming similar to him, and this can eliminate his aggressiveness. To identify with the aggressor means to accept his way of looking at the world.

However, the situation was different when the Japanese identified with westerners. As far as the Japanese were concerned, by identifying with westerners and by imitating their culture, they may have reduced the fear and anxiety of being exposed to the aggressor. But the Japanese gradually discovered that they were not accepted by the West, even though they thought they had become similar to the westerners.

The Japanese experienced this most decisively when Russia, France, and Germany strongly urged Japan to give up the Liaotung peninsula which Japan acquired from China as a result of the Sino-Japanese War. The Japanese government anticipated some opposition from Russia, but such strong pressure by the three countries was totally unexpected. This demand was made after the peace treaty was signed on 17 April 1895, and Japan was finally forced to return the peninsula to China.

This incident was a great shock to Japan's political thinkers as well as to the government. Japan had identified with the West and was trying hard to become just like a western country. But when the Japanese behaved like a colonising power, they were rejected by the very peoples with whom they had identified.

One of the most active and influential political thinkers and journalists of the time, Tokutomi Soho, wrote that he was angry not with Russia, France, and Germany, but with the Japanese diplomats who yielded to the three-nation demand. It is interesting to note here that he was not angry with the three European nations. This suggests that identification with the West was still very much in his mind at this point. However, this was a decisive event which changed his political view. He gradually began to advocate expansionism based on power and racism, as we shall see in the next chapter.

A conceivable psychoanalytic response upon discovering that the Japanese were rejected by the West was reaction formation. The envy and admiration for the West was turned into an emphasis on Japan and the East. Such an interpretation is possible from the writings of several thinkers of this period.

A good example is the case of Takayama Chogyu. He began to talk about a form of nationalism which he called 'Nihon shugi' ('Japanism'). In his opinion, westernisation had been taken to extremes, and now the Japanese were beginning to realise its harmful effects. Thus, in his own words, the 'extreme worship and imitation of foreign matters' created a 'violent reaction in the minds of the Japanese.' 'Japanism' emerged in order to 'explain the position of Japan in the world.'

The most important objective of Japanism, he continues, is to establish the most suitable practical principles of ethics for people and to unify public opinion in order to assure the people and to retain the independence and progress of Japan and the welfare and happiness of the Japanese. Japanism 'tries to realise the great ideal of building up Japan and to carry out the great ambition of our people.'

Since the Japanese are a 'basically colonising, conquering, and navigating people,' it was natural for him to visualise racial or ethnic confrontation in the future. In fact, this was seen by him as the competition between the Europeans and the Asians. He assumed that the 'final great struggle of racial competition' would take place in Japan.

In the case of another thinker Ukita Kazutami, Japan was in confrontation with Russia and in addition, a confrontation with the United States in the western hemisphere was possible. In his opinion, the world in the future would be divided into five regions by four or five superpowers.

The frustration resulting from the West's rejection was released onto the Chinese by way of displacement. It was noted that after the Sino-Japanese War, the Japanese suddenly began to despise the Chinese openly. As you will recall, the Japanese used to feel inferior to the Chinese for a long time, and as soon as the Japanese discovered that they had become more powerful than the Chinese, they seized the opportunity at once and began despising the Chinese. Finally, in 1937, Japan began to invade China.

Displacement was released against the Koreans as well. After the annexation of Korea in 1910, the Japanese began to colonise Korea extensively. A large number of Koreans were removed from their lands to Japan and were forced to work in coal mines and to do heavy construction work in extremely inhumane conditions. Count Okuma Shigenobu, who was also a politician and educator, insultingly wrote that the Koreans could become 'Japanese' if they could acquire the Japanese spirit.

Immediately after the Great Kanto Earthquake of 1923, many Koreans in Japan were massacred while others were arrested and kept in camps merely because of a rumour that they were planning to start a riot. Altogether more than 23,000 Koreans throughout Japan were 'protected' for up to two months.

6 Western Rejection and World War Two

FOLLOWING THE Sino-Japanese War of 1894-95, a war with Russia which would take place soon after was already anticipated by political thinkers. Yamaji Aizan, for example, thought that Japan must keep hold of China, and if Russia was intent on controlling China, too, Japan must look at Russia as the country to fight in the future.

When the war actually broke out in 1904, Mori Ogai, one of the leading novelists of the time, thought that if Japan won over Russia, anti-Asian feelings in the West would become intense. Mori had lived in the West, and he was quite familiar with the western intellectual climate. His prophesy was realistic enough and it turned out to be true. A large number of anti-oriental arguments were advanced after the war. This phenomenon was seen not only in the United States and Australia, where immigration of oriental workers was becoming a serious political issue, but also in those European countries in which such an issue was irrelevant.

Discrimination against the Japanese regarding emigration was another major factor in the Japanese realisation that their identification with the West was unwanted and therefore unsuccessful. If the rise of anti-Japanese feelings had been due purely to the fear of Japan becoming a future superpower, they were unlikely to have been discriminated against as immigrants. After all, Europeans of many nationalities were emigrating to the United States, Canada, and Australia, and not all of Europe was on friendly terms with these countries. Yet the immigrants from Europe were not discriminated against in the same sense the Japanese were.

The Japanese came to realise that they were rejected together with the Chinese because of their racial background. This realisation was a truly devastating and insulting blow. After all, the Japanese thought that they had become just like any other modern European nation that was expanding and colonising. By assuming the attitudes and ideology of the West, they had begun to look down on China as a backward country. But when the United States, Canada, or Australia handled the problem of immigration, the Japanese discovered that they were not regarded in any way as another 'western' nation. Instead, they were lumped together with the Chinese purely on the basis of racial classification.

This experience produced the following three reactions within Japan: (1) the denial of the oriental roots of the Japanese; (2) the acceptance of the western belief that the Japanese are inferior; and (3) the belief in the 'superiority of the Japanese race.'

Denial of Oriental Roots

The denial of Japan's oriental roots was expressed as a pseudo-science with several theories on the origin of the Japanese being proposed immediately after the outbreak of the Russo-Japanese War.

For example, in 1904, Taguchi Ukichi argued that the Japanese were actually 'Aryans,' pointing out that, unlike the Chinese, many Japanese had fine white skins. He seems to have confused race and language, and when he uses the term 'Aryans,' he seems to mean 'Caucasians', but he also seems to have meant the peoples speaking the Indo-European languages. As a result, Taguchi went to great lengths trying to show the significant differences between the Chinese language and the Japanese language. The point he wanted to make here was that the Japanese are different from the Chinese. His conclusion regarding the origin of the Japanese was that the Japanese belong to the same 'race' as the Indians, the Persians, and the Latins.

Another 'theory' was proposed by Kimura Takataro in 1913. According to him, the Japanese came from Senegal, Greece, and Egypt. As in the case of Taguchi, the basis for his argument is a comparison of languages. He tries to show that the Japanese language is similar to Greek, Latin, German, and English. According to him, one of the two writing systems in Japan, the *katakana,* was not derived from Chinese characters at all; it came from the Greek alphabet! He also points out that Japanese mythology is very similar to Greek mythology.

It is important to note here that these arguments were put forward when anti-Japanese feelings in Europe and America were being felt more and more in Japan. In fact, Taguchi states that because the Japanese are racially different from the Chinese and are the same as the peoples in India, Persia, Greece, and the Latin countries, to lump both the Chinese and the Japanese together and to discriminate against them equally is unjust.

Evidently, even Americans became aware of Japan's debate about origins, with the *New York Times* noting on 16 April 1913 that: 'There is small chance....that Japan will be able to maintain the assertion of an exclusively Aryan and Malay origin for the inhabitants of her island empire.' Nevertheless, attempts to deny their oriental roots persisted amongst some Japanese. In 1929, Oyabe Zenichiro argued that the Japanese were the descendants of the Gad; that is, one of the lost tribes of Israel! I might add that even in the 1970s and 1980s, similar types of pseudo-sciences can be found. Recently, I came across a book entitled (in translation) 'The Enigma of the Israeli Dynasty in Japan: The Truth of the Imperial Family' in a public library in Tokyo. The book was published in 1983.

Acceptance of 'Japanese Inferiority'

As a result of the intense anti-Japanese feelings in the West, another response was to accept the western view that all orientals are racially inferior. This is an understandable response because the Japanese consistently identified with westerners, and to take on the attitudes of the peoples they identified with was logical and natural.

For example, Count Okuma Shigenobu, a politician and educator, stated in a book that the Japanese were inferior to the Europeans. The skin colour of the Japanese was ugly, so were Japanese facial features, posture, and behaviour. The Japanese smiled too much without a reason. Like animals, they looked down instead of looking forward. They had not made any significant contributions in philosophy, religion, literature, or the arts. Racially and culturally, the Japanese were a second-rate people, said Okuma.

This book was published in 1913 — long after Japan's success in the Russo-Japanese War. In fact, many Japanese seemed to feel pessimistic about the future — a view expressed in several novels published at the time where the theme involved another war against Russia or a new war against the United States. As far as I can make out, Japan was usually defeated in these novels. For example, in 1913, Harada Masaemon, a lieutenant in the Imperial Japanese Army, published a novel in which Russia seeks her revenge against Japan and wins. The war was clearly conceived in racial terms, with the United States, the United Kingdom, and Russia cooperating. It is interesting to learn that a lieutenant wrote a novel like this, but at the same time, the novel also reveals how an officer in the Army thought about the future.

Belief in 'Japanese Superiority'

Yet another result was to reverse the feeling of inferiority and to insist on the 'superiority' of the Japanese in the form of reaction formation. After the Sino-Japanese War, as I mentioned earlier, the Japanese soon began to despise the Chinese and a similar change in attitude was observed towards the Russians, although to a lesser extent. Indeed, after the Russo-Japanese War, some Japanese began to think that the Russians were not superior to the Japanese after all.

Of the three responses that followed the Japanese realisation that they were rejected by the West, both the first and second alternatives did not continue to exist to any significant extent. In the case of the first alternative, the Japanese would have been obliged to keep insisting that they were not orientals, but such a notion was hard to believe even by the Japanese themselves.

The second alternative was to accept the racial inferiority of the Japanese as claimed by the West. However, many Japanese found such a view impossible to accept. The new ideology of Japanese expansionism had also developed already by this time, and such a belief was incompatible with this second alternative.

This means that the third alternative of reaction formation, insisting on the superiority of the Japanese, was the one which was less disturbing to the Japanese. Indeed, they gradually began to insist on the validity of this alternative. This ideology gained considerably more ground after World War I when the Japanese were forced to realise that they were rejected once again by the West.

Rise of Anti-Western Extremism

Japan decided against an active role in World War I as an ally of Great Britain, and, as it happened, was on the winning side. But anti-Japanese feelings in the West intensified further with Japan being seen as a growing power and a potential menace. As a result, the extent to which the Japanese reacted also increased considerably.

The existence of international tension and conflict in racial terms which was identified by many political activists and politicians alike became undeniable when the League of Nations was contemplated as a means of maintaining world peace after World War I. This was to be discussed at the peace conference in Paris in 1919, and the position the Japanese government held was that abolition of racial discrimination must be clearly included in the agreement among the future member nations before such an international body was formally constituted.

This proposal by the Japanese government was unanimously supported by Japanese politicians, and in 1919 over 300 people gathered at a meeting in Tokyo to agree a resolution in support of the government. The resolution was that racial discrimination was a source of international conflict, and without a ban on racial discrimination, any international organisation such as the League of Nations would be unable to function. If the representatives from various political parties are excluded, the overwhelming majority of the caucus members of this meeting were right-wing activists.

This clearly indicates that at this point, right-wing political ideology began to develop a formal tie with the formation of official policy of the Japanese government. I cannot emphasise the importance of this fact too much when we try to understand the history of World War II. Western rejection encouraged a rise in the belief in 'Japanese superiority,' which was the basis for most right-wing activists. As soon as their political and ideological ties with the Japanese government became established, right-wing extremists could influence and even control the policy of the Japanese government. This is exactly what took place. The Japanese government went to war in the Pacific because they followed the ideology of right-wing extremism.

At Paris, the Japanese proposal was violently opposed, especially by the Commonwealth nations, led by Australia. The delegates from Canada, New Zealand, and Australia argued, in effect, that if they should accept the Japanese as equals, they must also accept the Chinese and the Indians as equals as well, and that such a consequence was absolutely unacceptable. Prime Minister Hughes of Australia refused to discuss the matter any further and left the conference. The Japanese proposal was thus rejected.

It is important to note here that the anti-Japanese climate in the West was more or less instrumental in formally launching anti-western political extremism, combined with right-wing extremism and a belief in 'Japanese superiority,' in Japan. One of the most influential activists in this regard was Kita Ikki. He saw a class struggle between the nations of the world, with Great Britain and Russia in the role of 'capitalists,' while Japan occupied the role of 'proletariat.' He reasoned, therefore, that it is a natural right for a proletariat nation, such as Japan, to start a war against a country which monopolises huge territories unlawfully and ignores the universal law of coexistence of humanity both for the sake of self-defence and for the sake of a people oppressed by such an unjust power.

Here, he was advocating and justifying a war against Great Britain or the Soviet Union in order to acquire Australia or Siberia and also to help India become independent and to keep the western influence out of China. This idea was expressed in a publication entitled 'The Outline of the Principles for the Reform of the Nation' published in 1919; that is, after the Russian Revolution of 1917. This work was immediately banned because of its extreme position, but nevertheless, it was illegally printed and distributed underground. It was eagerly read by young officers in the military as the 'Bible' of the radical 'national reform' movement.

Here, he was advocating and justifying a war against Great Britain or the Soviet Union in order to acquire Australia or Siberia and also to help India become independent and to keep the western influence out of China. This idea was expressed in a publication entitled *Kokka Kaizoan Genri Taiko* ('The Outline of the Principles for the Reform of the Nation') published in 1919; that is, after the Russian Revolution of 1917. This work was immediately banned because of its extreme position, but nevertheless, it was illegally printed and distributed underground. It was eagerly read by young officers in the military as the 'Bible' of the radical 'national reform' movement.

Another activist, Okawa Shumei, presented a similar argument, but he placed more emphasis on the racial nature of the problem. According to him, Asians are not inferior to Europeans, but merely because the Europeans have been successful in the last 300 years or so, they dominate the world. But the 'coloured' peoples are awakening, and the Asians are to recover and to revive, he wrote.

When in 1924 the United States passed a law prohibiting immigration from Japan, this was seen as another fundamental racist attack on Japan and attracted violent anti-American feeling. The most notable example was when over 10,000 people gathered at a sports arena in central Tokyo for an anti-American meeting, and shouted: 'Start a war against America!'

Similar meetings were held in other cities in various parts of Japan. The Stars and Stripes at the American Embassy in Tokyo was dragged down to the ground. Many books discussing the future war against the United States began to appear, and organisations supporting such a war by looking at the nature of the problem racially were formed at about the same time.

The Japanese once again resorted to reaction formation. Since the Japanese thought they were being attacked on racial grounds, a further continuation of identification with the West could not solve the problem. To identify with the West and to take on the western attitude meant that they must accept western racism and the anti-Japanese immigration policy. However, this was not possible for two reasons.

First, the Japanese themselves felt that Japan was already an overcrowded country, and emigration was considered necessary. For example, the regional office of one of the political parties in Wakayama, the region of Japan from which a large number of Japanese had left for North America already, sent a formal letter to the Japanese delegates at the Paris conference in 1918. In this letter, the small habitable area of Japan, overcrowding, and the necessity of emigration were clearly stated.

Second, the acceptance of western racism was incompatible with the ideology of Japanese expansionism which already had developed extensively in the minds of influential political thinkers such as Takayama or Tokutomi. Since originally the ideology of Japanese expansionism developed as a result of the imitation of western expansionism and colonialism, as we have seen in the writing of Takayama, there was no logical inconsistency between identification with the West and Japanese expansionism.

But when the western ideology of racism became intense and was directed against the Japanese, an ideological incompatibility was evident. If the Japanese wanted to continue identifying with the West fully, then logically they must discriminate against themselves. However, if that was not possible, they must at least believe, as the West argued, that they were racially inferior and undesirable. If, on the other hand, the Japanese did not or could not think that they were racially inferior and undesirable, then they must discontinue the process of identification with the West forthwith.

Psychologists tell us that to have two incompatible ideas in our minds causes tension and stress and our natural reaction is to try to reduce or eliminate them. In a situation like this, one of the two incompatible ideas must be changed or modified in order to arrive at a less stressful state. For the Japanese, to continue identification with the West and to accept western racism was not possible due to the fully developed ideology of Japanese expansionism. Furthermore, this ideology was corroborated and strengthened by the outcomes of the wars against China and Russia, as well as of World War I. The logically acceptable way was to discontinue identification with the West which would then make it possible to reject western racism.

The Japanese solution was to retain the ideology of expansionism and colonialism and to combine this with the belief in Japanese superiority. Using this approach, expansionism and colonialism emerged as valid criteria for applying the conviction in Japanese superiority. And, as I stated earlier, the belief in Japanese superiority was a product of reaction formation where 'You are superior; you are wonderful' became 'We are superior; we are wonderful,' and 'We love you' became 'We hate you.'

Ideology for World War II

Indeed, reaction formation, which was already apparent after the Sino-Japanese and Russo-Japanese wars, became increasingly explicit. For example, in 1924, Ikuta Choko published an article entitled 'The Age of the Easterners is Coming.' In this work, he takes up the earlier ideology of the East versus the West. In his opinion, for a long time, the world was dominated by easterners, and that was a happy age. Westerners began to dominate the world only relatively recently, but already the surface of the earth has been contaminated by them. The easterners produced a large amount of culture and little civilisation, whereas the westerners created a large amount of civilisation and little culture. Therefore, the West is unhealthy. If easterners again control the world, the earth can be saved, he says.

In his opinion, to suggest the unification of the easterners against the westerners is not proper because that assumes the easterners are weak. The easterners are not weak. Then he states: '...the day when the easterners dominate the world once again will come soon. We easterners must regain our pride as easterners as soon as possible, and by means of our eastern culture, we must conquer the westerners.'

Ikuta is not especially racist when he expresses these ideas. For example, he thinks anti-Japanese attitudes in the United States are more a matter of the collision between two forms of capitalism than racial discrimination. But in the case of Tokutomi Soho, the perception of the problem is racial. In the article published in 1926 entitled 'Is the world going to be divided into two or three?' he says that the Japanese 'must be prepared to see the relationship between the white race versus the coloured races becoming more and more complicated, troublesome, and difficult in the future.'

He describes the unsuccessful identification with westerners in the following way: 'The results of pretending to be a people of the white race...are that, on the one hand, the Japanese are described by the Europeans and Americans as ape-like imitators, and on the other, the Japanese are looked upon enviously as traitors by the races in the East.' The beginning of reaction formation in his thought is seen in the following quotation. Tokutomi says:

'Shall we deal with the races in the East by presenting a new version of the dubious scientific hypothesis that the Japanese belong to the white race and by following them? Or shall we become the leading people of the world-wide equality movement by maintaining the pride of being one of the races in the East and as the core race among what the westerners call the "coloured races"? Which alternative shall we take? We need the most careful consideration here.'

Three years later, in 1929, his decision was clear. He says:

'Without paying attention to neighbouring countries, Japan must remain committed to the goal she aspired to. That is the ideal of the great imperial Japan. This ideal is to demonstrate the refined essence, namely the characteristics found uniquely in Japan, and to spread this throughout the world. In other words, this is to educate, to lead, and to improve the world by means of so-called cultural imperialism rather than military imperialism or economic imperialism. In other words, this means to supply the world with ethics, equality, freedom, peace, happiness, and humanism.'

The seeds of the anti-western ideology along with the seeds of the new ideology emphasising Japan's 'uniqueness' can be clearly identified in this statement.

The formation of various right-wing, race-concious organisations around this time was undoubtedly stimulated by the anti-Japanese attitudes of the West. For example, retired senior officers of the military founded an organisation called *Meirin Kai* (Association for Understanding Order) in 1932, which emphasised its aim, among others, 'to promote the right and prestige of the nation and to realise the principle of "the Great Asia."' Because of its close connection with the military, this organisation had a considerable impact on the military and its future.

Toa Renmei (The East Asian Alliance) was another such organisation, which had most influence on the military's decision to invade and subsequently administer north-east China (Manchukuo — 1931-1945). This society assumed that 'the decisive war between Imperial Japan and the Anglo-Saxons will be carried out in order to unify the civilisations of the world, and it might take place sooner than we expect.'

There were many organisations of this nature, but there were two principal organisations which had a direct impact on the future course of Japan's external policies. The first was called *Kokuhon Sha*, (Society for the Nation) which included the elites from both the military and government. The second was called *Seiten Kai* (The Blue Sky Society) which included many members from the *Kokuhon Sha*. Furthermore, *Seiten Kai* attracted many right-wing activists outside the military and government.

Inevitably, the fact that certain high officials in various government ministries were members of these organisations could mean that these anti-western, racist attitudes were gradually absorbed into official Japanese policies. Indeed, this is exactly what happened.

In 1938, the Japanese Government officially announced the formation of 'The New Order in East Asia,' in which the elimination of the western imperial powers from east Asia and the extermination of communism were among the stated objectives. This policy decision is extremely significant in the sense that the ideas which had been expressed by political activists, scholars, and journalists for a long time were finally given official shape and form by the Japanese government. This was soon followed by an expanded and more comprehensive plan called 'The Greater East Asia Co-prosperity Sphere,' in which even Australia and New Zealand were to be included. In these plans, the peoples of Asia were to be guided and directed by the Japanese, because of the 'superiority' of the Japanese. Under the direction of the Japanese, the peoples of Asia and the Pacific were to be liberated from western colonialism.

The principle objectives of this plan were officially expressed by the Ministry of Foreign Affairs and were in fact fully implemented — in the Japanese way. The massacres in Korea and China and in south-east Asia at the hands of the Japanese Armed Forces were comparable in extent and brutality to the Nazi 'holocaust' in Europe. Inasmuch as the Japanese were 'superior,' rationalisation was easy, in the same way that the Nazis justified their actions.

This was the situation in Japan before and during World War II. Towards the end of the war, more and more emphasis was placed on the sacred and divine nature of the Emperor, and Japan was described as the *shinshu* ('the Divine Land'). The Ministry of Education officially issued publications of this kind, and the dogma was imposed on school children as well as adults on a variety of occasions. To put it differently, the political ideology of racism, anti-western extremism, and colonialism, which was advocated by a relatively small number of activists earlier became the official ideology of the Japanese government and was taken even further. The Emperor became a living god, and Japan was sacred and divine. A country like this must win the war, the Japanese were told.

The reaction formation also became extreme. The attitude of 'You are superior; you are wonderful; we love you' became 'You are inferior; you are repugnant; we hate you,' and then this was advanced one step further. The Japanese began to argue that 'You are actually not human beings at all; you are beasts.' The expression *kichiku beiei* (devil beasts of America and Britain) was consistently used in newspapers. The war, the papers reported, was being fought between the *shimpei* (divine soldiers) of the Imperial Japanese forces and the 'devil beasts,' of the West.

7 Shock of the Defeat

AFTER LOSING a series of important battles in the Pacific (from the middle of 1942 onwards, beginning with the US victory at the Battle of Midway), it became increasingly obvious that Japan was going to be defeated sooner or later. It was only a matter of time. The military, the government, and the Emperor of Japan were very much aware of this. However, the military was sharply divided into two opposing factions. One faction thought that to continue a war which they could not possibly win would be futile, and that it would be better for the nation to plan for her survival and revival.

But the oppposing faction insisted that Japan must keep fighting, although they, too, knew full well that Japan could never win the war. This faction exploited slogans such as *Ichioku hinotama* (100 million Japanese as a fireball), *Ichioku gyokusai* (100 million Japanese will fight and die), and *hondo kessen* (the last and decisive battle on the main islands). Applying the technique mentioned earlier, each slogan consisted of four Chinese characters. This group even argued that children, the aged and the sick must be killed before the forthcoming *hondo kessen*.

However, the two atomic bombs over Japan (Hiroshima on 6 August and Nagasaki on 9 August) forced the Emperor to respond immediately and make his desire to end the war clear and to do so publicly. Thus, his verbal statement at a meeting on 10 August 1945 was written down by the Chief Cabinet Secretary. His draft was discussed, modified, and edited at the cabinet meeting on 14 August and was finally made official. This became the Emperor's rescript regarding the acceptance of the Joint Declaration of the Allied Powers. There was no question but that the rescript was admitting Japan's defeat in the war. Of course, the opposing faction was violently against such a proclamation, which was to be delivered over the radio by the Emperor himself. Assassinations and assassination attempts as well as an attempt to prevent the Emperor's broadcast took place, hence, for security reasons, the rescript was first recorded on a 78 rpm disc.

Upon Hearing the News of Defeat

The recording of the Emperor's statement was finally broadcast over the radio at noon on 15 August 1945. This was the first time the Japanese had ever heard the Emperor's voice. To many people, this fact itself was incredible. The quality of the recording, however, was very poor and the language used by the Emperor was archaic and totally unintelligible to most Japanese. Nevertheless, they could more or less infer what he was trying to say. The rescript read as follows:

'We declared war on America and Britain out of Our sincere desire to ensure Japan's self-preservation and the stabilisation of East Asia. It was not Our intention... to infringe upon the sovereignty of other nations or to seek territorial aggrandisement.

'...The enemy has begun to employ a new and cruel bomb...Should We continue to fight, the ultimate result would be not only the obliteration of the race but the extinction of human civilisation. Then, how should We be able to save the millions of Our subjects and make atonement to the hallowed spirits of Our Imperial Ancestors? This is why we have commanded the Imperial Government to comply with the terms of the Joint Declaration of the powers.'

This is the official English version as received by the Allied Forces. Since the Japanese version was so difficult to understand to ordinary Japanese, it sounded more like a ritual of ending the war than a communication.

Immediately after the Emperor's broadcast, several forms of behaviour were observed. In social psychology, it is known that when a person is exposed to bad news, he or she goes through a series of psychological states. For example, following the assassination of President Kennedy in 1963, the most common types of reaction among Americans followed a well-defined pattern of grief: (a) an initial phase of shock and disbelief; (b) a developing awareness of the loss accompanied by feelings of sadness, sorrow, shame, and anger; (c) the onset of physical symptoms such as tears, tenseness, a sleeplessness, fatigue, and loss of appetite; and (d) a gradual recovery. Judging from the contemporary descriptions in newspapers and other publications, it appears that the Japanese experienced similar responses after the Emperor's broadcast.

Up until that moment, despite the routine air raids day and night, many Japanese were misled by the mass media which were completely controlled by the military government and believed in Japan's ultimate victory in the war. As a result, they did not feel they were defeated. But after the rescript was broadcast, the fact of the defeat was accepted by most Japanese, and various emotional reactions are on record. Some people were angry with the government and the military. Several letters suggesting suicide were sent to General Tojo, who was generally considered responsible for starting the war against the United States. In public, there were numerous occasions when people called out to him: 'Why don't you commit suicide?'

Some Japanese were angry with the Emperor and with the content of his broadcast. For example, Hotta Yoshie, a novelist, wrote: 'What kind of a man are you? Is that all you have to say? Do you think you can be forgiven?' He recalls how, after completing the sentence, he was then shaken with a mixed feeling of anger and sadness.

However, weeping appears to have been the most widely observed phenomenon. Already in the afternoon of 15 August, many people gathered in the square in front of the Emperor's palace in Tokyo, and they wept in large numbers. No information was given as to the approximate number of people who went there to weep, but 'many more than 200 people' were seen marching towards the square by a newspaper reporter. People remained there, wept for a while, and then went away, while different people came and repeated the same behaviour. This phenomenon was seen repeated many times.

It is possible that at least some of them went there because they felt responsible for the defeat. They also went there so that they could feel close to the Emperor emotionally. They then wanted to apologise to the Emperor because they did not win the war. But because they were overwhelmed with feelings of sadness and sorrow, they began to weep. At least, it is fair to say that this interpretation can certainly be drawn from the newspaper reports. For example, the *Asahi Shinbun* writes:

"'Forgive us, Your Majesty." "Your Majesty!" Painful cries were heard here and there. One young man stood up and shouted from the top of his voice: "Your Majesty, *Banzai!*"'

A reporter for the *Asahi Shinbun* writes:

'I held a pebble [in the square] in my hand firmly and shouted; "Your Majesty...please forgive..." but I could not continue...

'I stood up and shouted: "Everybody...we have no way of apologising to His Majesty..." After that, I was unable to say any more. "I am also one of His Majesty's subjects." "No matter what happens after this..." Then this voice was overshadowed by a fit of intense weeping.'

There were also other Japanese, of course, who reacted differently to Japan's defeat. They saw the end of the war as a liberation from the hard life they had experienced during the war. For example, one intellectual who had been against the war was happy to see the beginning of a new life. He writes: 'I became overwhelmed by the feeling of happiness. This is not a dream, this is not a dream! The war is over!'

Suicide was the most extreme consequence upon hearing the news of the defeat. Already on 14 August, immediately after the cabinet meeting held in front of the Emperor, in which the acceptance of the Joint Declaration was announced by the Emperor, General Anami, Minister of the Army, committed *seppuku* (often called *harakiri* incorrectly) at his official residence. In his will, he stated: 'I would like to apologise for the great crime by offering a death [of mine].' By this, he meant that he was responsible for the unsuccessful result of the war, and 'the great crime' here refers to the processes leading to the defeat in the war. In his will, he also stated: 'I believe in the invincibility of the Divine Land [Japan]. Since I am blessed by the grace from His Majesty, I have not a single word to leave [in this world].'

According to the *Mainichi Shinbun* dated 29 August 1945, by that day, a total of 35 civilians had committed suicide. Most of them were around 20 years old. The newspaper states that 'they felt responsible for the poor performance of duty and apologised to the Emperor by means of their deaths.'

On 12, 13, and 14 September two former cabinet ministers and two generals in the military committed suicide. Similarly, officers of lower ranks in the military committed suicide in various parts of Japan. General Tojo bungled a later attempt at suicide and was subsequently hanged as a war criminal in 1948.

Defence Mechanisms

Since the shock of the defeat was overwhelming and truly traumatic to the Japanese, there was an urgent need to adjust psychologically. Judging from the information given in newspapers and other contemporary publications, it is possible to infer several defence mechanisms in the minds of the Japanese.

Denial. At first, many Japanese did not believe the news, and this was especially true in the countryside. Even after the news of the defeat itself was accepted, its content was distorted and was made less painful. For example, in one area in Fukui Prefecture, the 'unconditional surrender' which the Japanese government agreed upon as the official form of accepting the defeat was considered the best and most advantageous way to end the war. It was believed that 'unconditional surrender' meant that Japan would not have to pay indemnification. The Japanese commonly used the expressioin *shusen* ('the end of the war') rather than *haisen* ('the defeat in the war').

The same tendency for denial was already seen in the Emperor's rescript accepting the Joint Declaration. It stated that it was not intended to interfere with the independence of other countries and to invade them. Here, the large-scale invasions by the Imperial Japanese forces and atrocities they committed all over Asia are completely denied. The reason for starting a war against the United States and Great Britain is described as 'self-defence.' Also, the word 'surrender' itself is carefully avoided. The important facts in the objective world are all denied.

An influential newspaper the *Yomiuri Hochi* printed the following editorial on 15 August 1945:

'...The Greater East Asian War [World War II in the Pacific]...has been a war of justice as well as a war of self-defence and self-preservation. The objective of the war has been the liberation of East Asia and peace and the welfare of a billion people...It was intended to contribute to peace in the world and the progress of mankind by establishing eternal peace in East Asia. There was no intention to seek monopoly or the acquisition of territories.'

Here, the author repeats the content of the Emperor's rescript and adds a little more to it. The war is described as a war of 'justice.' The peoples in East Asia were to be 'liberated,' and they were to have 'peace and welfare.'

The same mechanism of denial continued to exist. Even after the Japanese were faced with the reality of seeing the soldiers of the Allied Powers in Japan, the Japanese called them *shinchugun* ('advance forces') and they almost never used the expression *senryogun* ('occupation forces').

Isolation. American journalists who arrived in Japan with the occupation forces immediately after the capitulation reported repeatedly that the Japanese were emotionless or apathetic. For example, F.L. Kluckhohn, a correspondent for the *New York Times*, writes: '...from our huge C-54 Skymaster, we looked down a few hundred feet on roads on which Japanese walked or cycled without even bothering to look up as the planes passed over them...'

An anonymous journalist for the *New York Times* thought that the adult Japanese were apathetic while the children were cheerful. Mark Gayn, another journalist for the *Chicago Sun Times*, felt that the Japanese seemed not to care.

Ensign O'Connell wrote in his diary his impression of the Japanese as of September, 1945 as follows: 'All of them looked like scarecrows — they looked upon us with neither fear nor hostility nor — anything. Their eyes were blank, and if spoken to they came to and would smile in a contorted way which I have learned does not connote mirth to them.' I think this brief statement is an excellent description of isolation. The contorted 'smile' might be interpreted as an expression of reaction formation, because Japanese culture encourages a person to smile, laugh, and joke in a variety of stressful situations.

Rationalisation. This defence mechanism is also seen in the Emperor's rescript. It says that the reason for accepting the Joint Declaration is to avoid the extermination of the Japanese and the destruction of human civilisation by the atomic bomb. It further states that if such an outcome takes place, the Emperor cannot apologise to the spirits of his ancestors. Here, the impact of the invention of the atomic bomb is extended to the whole human race, and in this way, the act of accepting the Joint

Declaration is explained as a justification and is made less painful.

In the *Asahi Shinbun* editorial of 15 August 1945, rationalisation is also evident. It states:

'...The liberation of the oppressed races, the true spirit of the Declaration of the Greater East Asia in which the rebuilding of ethnic nations without exploitation and enslavement, and the realisation of the suicide missions which are unique to our country are all honourable products of the Greater East Asian War...and these spirits must be written about eternally as the beautiful fruits of our nationality...'

On the following day, another rationalisation appeared in the *Asahi Shinbun*:

'...The result of this war probably...lies in the great contribution towards the awakening of Asia...The fact that the great majority of the races in East Asia willingly cooperated with us clearly indicates how strong their desire for freedom and liberation was...We believe consistently that the only way to save Asia is to unite Asia...'

Most Asians who suffered from Japanese invasion, colonialism, torture, and atrocity would say that these statements are outright lies. I agree. In order to rationalise, even journalists must write like this. I should add that the *Asahi Shinbun* has always been one of the most influential newspapers in Japan, and many Japanese believe that this newspaper is the most reliable, accurate, and conscientious daily newspaper in Japan. Other newspapers resorted to very much the same kind of editorial rhetoric.

Intellectualisation. A tendency for this defence mechanism may be recognised as well. A professor at the University of Tokyo made the following comments in the *Asahi Shinbun* on 16 August 1945: 'Japan has been based on the interrelationships between man, nature, and god. This is based on Harmony, and power of this Harmony has been the driving force to overcome many national difficulties...' The expression is very abstract and you probably do not understand what he is saying here, but to many Japanese, to think like this might have helped them to detach themselves from the reality around them.

Beginning of the Occupation

The Japanese tried to resist the Occupation as much as possible — not least the Ministry of Foreign Affairs. It stated that Japan was ready to pay the full price of defeat but that the Japanese would 'react' if treated too severely. A ministry spokesman, speaking officially, said: 'Stevenson said it takes two to make a kiss. It also takes two to make friendship. Japan is ready on her part.'

On 5 September 1945, in his address to the Diet, Prime Minister Higashikuni said: 'It is the duty of us all to conform absolutely with the Imperial command' without mentioning the existence of General MacArthur. There were great cheers when one of the congressmen said: 'If there are any illegal acts on the part of the Allies we must rectify them.' Because of these Japanese attitudes, the 24 September issue of *Newsweek* magazine demanded that Japan must behave like a defeated country.

When they were not resorting to defence mechanisms, the ordinary Japanese were either hostile or bitter towards the Americans, according to F.L. Kluckhohn of the *New York Times*. He describes how he and Gordon Walker of the American Broadcasting Company were treated by the Japanese:

'We tried to hail several cabs but were ignored...We walked into a bank, where we asked if anyone spoke English. We received...glares and were ignored. We walked about a block and then saw a man entering a small car with a chauffeur. We requested, with as much an air of authority as we could muster, that he drive us to the Imperial Hotel. He acceded but refused to talk with us. The "cold treatment" thereafter alternated during the long day with complaints as to the way our bombers had acted.'

Kluckhohn also recounts how the Japanese kept ignoring the Americans, and even when General MacArthur arrived at the American Embassy officially, 'only a handful of the Tokyo residents watched the parade, and none gathered near the Embassy.' He and Gordon Walker saw 'peasants turn their backs to ignore' them. They saw 'hostile eyes' everywhere. Two nuns — one English and one French — were worried if it was safe for them to travel in a United States uniform.

8 General MacArthur: The New Emperor From America

GENERAL MacArthur arrived in Japan on 30 August 1945, and on 2 September on board the battleship *USS Missouri* in the Bay of Tokyo, Japan's formal surrender took place. The Occupation had begun. But it appears that the occupation forces felt the Japanese did not take the fact of occupation seriously. The *New York Times* wrote on 2 September as follows:

'[Japanese officers] appeared to have accepted the fact of defeat. Whether they realised its full implications was a question...[I]t was noted that they seemed to feel no humility or remorse, that a good proportion of them appeared to think that now the game of war was over bygones should be bygones.'

It is impossible to know how the Japanese officers described above actually thought and felt, but the Americans did obtain a certain impression of the Japanese, who did not behave like a defeated people as the Americans had expected. This perception was in a sense substantiated, for example, by the attitudes shown by the Japanese government as well as the Diet — as I mentioned in the preceding chapter.

Japanese newspapers also showed a defiant attitude towards the occupation forces. The Japan Broadcasting Corporation (NHK), which was totally controlled by the government, continued to broadcast news about alleged crimes committed by the soldiers of the occupation forces on its short-wave overseas broadcasts. Japanese newspapers consistently used the expression *kosho* (negotiation) in order to refer to the communications between the occupation forces and the Japanese government. This was a source of great irritation to SCAP (Supreme Commander for the Allied Powers, although the initials came to stand for the entire administration of the occupation forces).

MacArthur Over and Above the Emperor

In order to overrule the policy of the Japanese government and to control Japanese journalism, SCAP assumed a strong authoritarian position which was made very clear to the Japanese. On 4 September, for example, NHK's overseas broadcasts were banned. On 9 September, MacArthur announced his policy of administering Japan by restricting freedom of speech and by exercising press censorship.

On 15 September his policy was conveyed to Japanese journalists at a press conference by Colonel Donald Hoover. The following points were made very clear to the Japanese and were printed in Japanese newspapers on 17 September. Namely: (1) General MacArther wants the Japanese people to understand clearly that Japan is never going to be considered an equal with the Allied Powers in any conceivable way whatsoever; (2) Japan will not be permitted the right to occupy any position among the civilised nations; (3) Japan is a defeated country; (4) There can be no negotiations between them; and (5) The Supreme Commander-in-Chief orders the Japanese government, and they do not negotiate because negotiation is possible only between equals.

In this way, the Japanese were forced to realise the extent of the power and authority MacArthur exercised over them. MacArthur also impressed the Japanese by refusing to see them as much as possible and maintained a distance from them. I might add here that this policy reminds us of Commodore Perry who kept insisting on seeing officials of the highest rank only. Not only that, both Perry and MacArthur thought that the display of power was the best way to deal with the Japanese. The American love for power and power display and the Japanese tendency for identification with the aggressor turned out to be complementary to each other again in this case, as I shall explain shortly.

In contrast to MacArthur's exercise of power, the Emperor's

power declined significantly in the eyes of the Japanese. First of all, the relative power of the relationship between General MacArthur and the Emperor was made abundantly clear and decisive when the Emperor visited General MacArthur for the first time on 27 September.

On 29 September, newspapers printed a picture showing them together, and anyone who saw this picture clearly recognised a vast difference in power status between the two men. The facial expression and posture each man showed were extremely revealing. MacArthur looked relaxed and casual, but the Emperor appeared tense and formal. In this picture, the non-verbal comunication each man conveyed to the average Japanese told of the downfall of the old Emperor and the emergence of a new 'emperor' from the United States.[1]

Indeed, because of the immense symbolic significance of this picture, the Japanese Ministry of Foreign Affairs thought that it was a disgrace and instructed the newspapers not to print it. However, the General Headquarters of the Allied Powers (GHQ) overruled this order and the picture was printed the following day. The Emperor also stated officially that he was not a 'god in a human form,' and newspapers wrote about him and his family living in a defeated country like any other Japanese.

In this way, the Japanese were forced to learn that MacArthur was the *de facto* head of Japan over and above the Emperor. He began to be called 'the moat-side emperor' because his office, in the Dai Ichi Seimei building (the former premises of an insurance company), was near the moat of the Imperial Palace. MacArthur received approximately 1,000 letters each month from Japanese throughout the country; one letter called MacArthur 'the greatest man in the world,' while another urged him to bring his family to Japan and become their president.

Although MacArthur did display his authority and power over the lives of the Japanese, the Japanese did not seem to develop negative reactions towards the Occupation. The reason seems to have been that, in the eyes of the Japanese, there were far fewer atrocities than expected. Those who were familiar with the atrocities committed by the Japanese forces in various parts of Asia during the war were prepared to see similar actions by the soldiers of the Allied Powers.

To the surprise of the Japanese, however, the absolute power held by the occupation forces was not abused by exploiting or taking advantage of the civilian population. This created a favourable impression of the occupation forces amongst the Japanese. The Japanese reaction was so favourable, in fact, that as early as September 1945 General MacArthur issued an official statement saying that the total manpower level of the occupation forces could be reduced to 200,000 men by 1 July 1946. Naturally, a positive major policy decision of this kind helped considerably in persuading the Japanese to accept the occupation forces as the possessors of legitimate power in their country.

MacArthur as a Symbolic Father Figure

It appears that the Japanese began to perceive MacArthur as a symbolic father figure some time after the realisation of the vast power difference between MacArthur and the Emperor. Basically, there were two important reasons why this happened.

First, the Japanese have a tendency to perceive a relationship based on authority in terms of a parent-child relationship. To put it differently, authority relationship within Japanese society is often seen as a symbolic extension of the parent-child relationship. This phenomenon is seen, for example, between employer and employees, gangster boss and his followers, or teacher and students.

The relationship between the Emperor and ordinary Japanese was another example. Until the end of the war, the Emperor had the absolute and highest authority, and the Japanese were told that their relations with the Emperor were the extension of the parent-child relationship in the most dignified form. It was emphasised that this relationship was the foundation of Japan as a nation.

This idea of 'the Emperor as the father of Japan' was to be found more or less in all forms of right-wing extremism, and was later taken up officially by the military government. Japanese soldiers were told to fight and to die for the Emperor, who was the benevolent father of the great family that was Japan.

When the war ended, newspapers described the Japanese as 'babies' taken care of by the Emperor. For example, on 16 August 1945, the influential *Asahi Shinbun* wrote: '…The Emperor was benevolently interested in the babies' lives during the war and in their effort to increase food production…One of the reasons why [His Majesty] decided to accept the terms of the Joint Declaration seems to be that [His Majesty] did not wish to intensify the disaster for the innocent babies any further.' The crowds in front of the Emperor's palace on the day of defeat were also described as 'babies' by the same newspaper.

Another influential newspaper, the *Mainichi Shinbun*, wrote as follows on 21 August 1945: 'There was no baby which did not weep with a feeling of awe upon hearing His Majesty's voice [over the radio]...How did the Japanese understand the fact that [His Majesty] explained...as if an honourable and benevolent father were teaching his children?'

Some Japanese tried to explain their relationship with the Emperor to MacArthur. For example, one letter said: '[Until the end of the war] the Emperor was considered a parent and...ordinary Japanese were considered children.' When the former allied countries began to discuss the possibility of prosecuting the Emperor as a war criminal, MacArthur received letters against it. For example, one letter said: 'The Emperor is not a war criminal. The Emperor is the father of us Japanese nationals.'

Second, there was a complementary attitude of paternalism on the part of MacArthur. In his *Reminiscences*, he expresses this attitude often. For example, he writes: 'I had a deep responsibility as guardian of these people so dramatically brought under my charge.' MacArthur seemed to have an intense sense of mission to reform Japan completely. In his own words, Japan had become 'the world's greatest laboratory for an experiment in the liberation of a people from totalitarian military rule and for the liberalisation of government from within.' On the basis of this perception of his role in occupied Japan, MacArthur says: 'I was determined that our principles during the occupation would be the same principles for which our soldiers had fought on the battlefield.'

Paternalistic Occupation Policy

The policy of the occupation forces as experienced by the Japanese was in agreement with their perception of themselves and of MacArthur, and to them, MacArthur approached his responsibilities as if he were taking care of weak, dependent, and incompetent children. One of the first things the occupation forces did which greatly impressed the Japanese concerned food supplies. When the Imperial Japanese forces occupied other countries, they always expected the native population to feed the Japanese troops regardless of any local food shortages.

For this reason, the Japanese naturally assumed that they would have to feed the occupation troops despite a critical food shortage throughout Japan at the time of the surrender. In anticipation of this 'food for the troops' requirement, the Kanagawa prefectural authorities, for example, had set aside a store of onions, potatoes, fruit, and meat ready for the occupation forces.

However, as soon as MacArthur became aware of the complete exhaustion of Japanese food resources, he issued an order forbidding the occupation forces to eat local Japanese food. Instead, food for all military personnel was brought in from the United States. Not only that, the occupation forces also offered surplus food to the Japanese. Later, a large-scale food relief programme was undertaken.

The Japanese responded by expressing their gratitude officially to General MacArthur. Emperor Hirohito is said to have expressed his personal gratitude, with tears in his eyes saying that the Japanese considered General MacArthur as the 'Divine Wind.' Here, the expression 'Divine Wind' can be considered to mean 'divine assistance.' Similarly, in the Lower House of the Diet, on 5 July 1947, members approved a resolution to express gratitude to MacArthur.

Another major policy decision which was implemented by the occupation forces (which at the same time was entirely consistent with Japanese perception of their relationship with MacArthur) was the democratisation of Japanese society. Within a very short time, the virtues of democracy, and the necessity of becoming a democratic country were being taught in schools throughout the land, while the population as a whole was instructed on the same virtues through the mass media. Here, the Americans were projected as the model of a desirable human being, and the Japanese were taught and encouraged to become like them. Similarly, it was official policy to identify with the Americans and the explicit intention to change Japan into a western-type democracy — at least outwardly.

To many Japanese who had suffered under the military and totalitarian government before and during the war, this policy appeared very attractive and wonderful and General MacArthur was seen as a liberator. Political or religious freedom, freedom of speech, the liberation of women and equality of the sexes, and land reform were very welcome changes to the oppressed

Japanese. Indeed, when Japanese workers were allowed to celebrate May Day for the first time after the war in 1946, they expressed their gratitude to the occupation forces at a mass gathering in Tokyo.

Regression

As far as I can see, the Japanese did not seem to show any defensive behaviour which could be interpreted as regression immediately after the end of the war. But as time went on, signs of regression emerged. As I mentioned earlier, the Japanese tend to look at a relationship based on authority as an extension of the parent-child relationship. As a result, as soon as they accepted General MacArthur as the possessor of legitimate power and authority over them, they were ready to accept him as a symbolic father figure.

Since MacArthur perceived himself as a guardian of the Japanese and in fact carried out a paternalistic occupation policy, the Japanese perception and expectation of MacArthur as 'father' were fully substantiated. It would appear that this encouraged the Japanese to fulfil their role as 'children' more overtly. For example, the Japanese began to write letters to MacArthur as their symbolic father. One woman wrote: '...now Japan is just a little baby in democratic life, you see.' Another letter stated that the majority of the Japanese were still children and asked him not to expect too much. I think these expressions are extremely important as regards the Japanese inferring a change in the personification of their symbolic father. Clearly, MacArthur had taken over the position of 'father,' which had been previously held by the Emperor.

Conceivably, the image of MacArthur as a symbolic father became clearer as time went by, and for their part, the Japanese thought and felt like his 'children.' When MacArthur was abruptly released from his post by President Truman, Japan's leading newspapers all published very similar editorials in the morning edition of 12 April 1951. They all revealed unmistakable regression signals. For example, the *Asahi Shinbun* stated:

'...It was General MacArthur who taught us the virtues of democracy and pacifism and kindly led us to this hopeful way [of life]. It was also General MacArthur who was happy to see...the Japanese moving towards democracy step by step as if he were enjoying the growth of a child and he constantly encouraged us to do so...

'...The foundation of the direction towards democracy instilled in the minds of the Japanese will not change. We will continue to walk the same road even more vigorously by simply following the same direction.'

The *Mainichi Shinbun* editorial was very similar:

'The General came to Japan not as a conqueror but as a great reformer...He gave us an ideology called "freedom and dignity of the individual" which was new to the Japanese and [he] made us understand it...The General loved and trusted the Japanese...We Japanese loved and trusted the General...Our love and trust for the General will not change. The best way for us Japanese to express our gratitude to the General...is to exist in accordance with his trust.'

Yet another influential newspaper, the *Yomiuri Shinbun,* published the following editorial:

'Towards the Japanese citizens...he offered caressing hands instead of a blow by iron fists...No one will object if we thank General MacArthur as the benefactor in the rebirth of Japan...We should proceed towards democracy without losing trust for the United States, and this will make General MacArthur most happy.'

These editorials are informative in that they describe the psychological relationship between General MacArthur and the Japanese as seen by them until the day of his dismissal. The recovery of Japan after the war is described as 'the growth of a child' and the policy of the occupation forces is described as 'the offer of caressing hands.' Here, the Japanese are compared to a small and incompetent child who must be protected and raised.

In contrast, General MacArthur is seen as a protector who can teach virtues such as democracy and peace, as well as freedom and dignity of the individual. The relationship between General MacArthur and the Japanese is seen as a loving and trusting one which is not going to change. Here, a relationship of permanence as found, for example, among kith and kin, is assumed. The Japanese are encouraged to move towards democracy and even after his departure for the United States, the Japanese are supposed to follow his direction. In this way, the Japanese can express their gratitude to him and make him happy.

The essential idea expressed in these remarkably similar

editorials is the notion of General MacArthur and the Japanese having the relationship of a parent and child. A child is protected and raised by a thoughtful parent who teaches the child the proper way to be a human being. The child feels grateful to the parent and behaves according to the parent's standard and values even when the parent is away.

I should add that press censorship was officially lifted in 1948, and newspapers, therefore, could publish freely in 1951, at least in theory. Nevertheless, it is arguable that Japanese journalists had to be circumspect about what they wrote and how they expressed themselves even in 1951. But why did they use the parent-child metaphor? They could have written an editorial from any number of different angles without offending the occupation forces or the Japanese government or General MacArthur himself. The fact that they wrote in the way they did clearly shows regression in the minds of the Japanese.

There is an additional story to this incident. MacArthur returned to America, and from 3-5 May 1951 he was summoned to the joint hearing by the Senate Armed Services and Foreign Relations Committees. At this hearing, MacArthur stated that the IQs of the Japanese were at about the level of 12-year-old children. This remark soon became widely known and more or less accepted among the Japanese.

Identification with the Aggressor

In a defeated country where the occupation forces control almost every aspect of life, one conceivable defence mechanism we would expect is identification with the aggressor. But as far as I can see, this defence mechanism did not emerge immediately after the Occupation. As we have seen in the preceding chapter, a variety of defence mechanisms were observed after the surrender, but identification with the aggressor was absent.

Another defence mechanism which was not observed immediately after the surrender and the beginning of the Occupation was regression. Both regression and identification with the aggressor developed gradually through time. It is very interesting to note that in the Nazi concentration camps, it took several years for the prisoners to develop identification with the Gestapo, and according to Bettelheim who observed them carefully from the inside, this defence mechanism emerged only after they had been forced to behave like children. That is, first they were forced to regress, and then they began to identify with the Gestapo (see Appendix, pp. 142-144).

The same sequence of events were observed in Japan after the war. First, the Japanese dealt with the shock of defeat and the beginning of the Occupation by means of a variety of defence mechanisms except regression and identification with the aggressor. But the occupation forces treated the Japanese, in effect as 'children' by enforcing a paternalistic occupation policy. As a result, the Japanese regressed. It was after this that they began to show identification with the aggressor.

I hope you do not misunderstand the point I am making here. I am not trying to say that the occupation forces treated the Japanese like the Gestapo. I am not saying occupied Japan was like a concentration camp. What I am saying is that both in the concentration camp and occupied Japan, the people involved realised that they were being treated like children. Although the method of making them feel so was quite different, the effect was rather similar. Upon realising that they were being treated like children, they regressed in both cases. Indeed, they were encouraged to regress. In the same way, after regression, they began to identify with the aggressor in both cases.

In occupied Japan, both adults and children began to identify with MacArthur. For example, in the issue of 11 July 1983, *Newsweek* describes how the Japanese looked upon MacArthur during the Occupation. One woman recalls: 'I remember "playing MacArthur" with my friends. Everybody wanted to play the role of the general, but no one even talked about the emperor.' This was how Japanese children played at that time.

Among the letters MacArthur received from Japanese, there were ones from women asking him to father their babies. Although this desire may imply that these women wanted to marry MacArthur, it would be more correct to say that they wanted to be the mothers of children fathered by him. That is, they wanted to see MacArthur through the eyes of children, placing themselves at their level. In Japan, as in many other cultures, what anthropologists call 'teknonymy' is practised; this is when a woman often calls her husband 'father' or 'daddy' and vice versa, even when they are childless. This practice as well as their perception of themselves as 'children' probably made the Japanese women write such letters.

Identification with MacArthur went even further. A rumour began to be spread that MacArthur was part-Japanese. The story related how his great grandmother had been a Japanese woman born in Kyoto, while another version told of how his mother was Japanese and that he grew up in Japan until he was six. Other rumours said that Arthur MacArthur, the General's son, would marry a Japanese princess when he grew up, or that MacArthur had a daughter who was unknown to the Japanese and she, too, might marry into Imperial circles.

These rumours are remarkable in two ways. First, the stories suggest a symbolic merging of the Japanese and the MacArthurs in the minds of the Japanese. And second, the family of the former father figure, namely the Imperial family, and the family of the new father figure, namely the MacArthurs, are merged. By this means, identification with the aggressor as a defence mechanism could serve the purpose by decreasing the difference between the Japanese and the Americans and also by equating the two father figures.

Along with such a process, identification with the Americans in general was also conceivable, and indeed the documents from that period are informative. As I already mentioned, many Japanese wrote letters to MacArthur — in English as well as Japanese; one letter in English said: 'When America fight with any other country every young people of Japan naturally stand and join American army as volunteers [sic].' A boy who wanted to become a US citizen wrote that he had 'absolute no Japanese spirit [sic]' and he was 'yankeefied [sic].' Many Japanese said that Japan should be allowed to join America as one of the States, while others suggested that Japan should become an American territory.

The desire to become a part of the United States was expressed not only by ordinary Japanese in the street, but also by more influential Japanese. For example, Kume Masao, a novelist, wrote an article entitled *Nihon Beishu Ron* ('Japan as One of the States of America') in a magazine called *Sekai Shunjyu* in the February issue, 1950. He argued that the Japanese would be happier if Japan could join America as the 49th state.[2]

Identification with the Americans could also be seen in Japanese behaviour. One of the most striking American behavioural traits the Japanese noticed was the use of chewing gum. But since chewing gum was not available to Japanese, some

Japanese imitated Americans by chewing dried squid (traditional Japanese food), pretending to have chewing gum in their mouths. Of course, the Japanese soon began to produce chewing gum themselves, and the manufacturers made a fortune. Another American behavioural trait the Japanese imitated was to cross their legs when seated.

However, due mainly to racial differences, it was not easy for most Japanese to 'pass' for Americans, but they still could try to 'pass' for Japanese Americans. In fact, some Japanese began to imitate their mannerisms and language, and tried very hard to pass for Japanese Americans. Native Japanese men pretended to be Japanese Americans by speaking Japanese with an American accent and approached Japanese women. In this way, the same Japanese men suddenly became sexually attractive to Japanese women! In fact, women were often sexually exploited by these men. Many cases of fraud also involved fake Japanese Americans, because it was easier to deceive Japanese this way.

One of the well-known criminal cases during the Occupation involved two teenagers; a 19-year-old boy and an 18-year-old girl. When they were arrested after a robbery, they pretended to be Japanese Americans by speaking only English; or to be more exact, by trying to make others feel that they were speaking English. Apparently, they consistently behaved in this way when in the company of other Japanese.

9 Japanese Literature

IN THE PRECEDING chapters, I have tried to look at Japanese history from a psychoanalytical point of view. I hasten to add, however, that the reader should not imagine I have covered all the major events in Japanese history. Obviously, there were important events which had nothing whatsoever to do with defence mechanisms. I set out to try to inform the reader about three very important facts in Japanese history which concern defence mechanisms. These are (1) the impact of the continental cultures upon Japan; (2) the impact of the West, especially since the middle of the nineteenth century; and (3) the defeat in World War II. I think Japanese responses to these three facts are important enough to shape, modify, or even determine the character of Japanese culture. This is the essence of my book.

I shall now review some Japanese literary works. Please note, however, that only those works which are relevant to the discussions presented in the preceding chapters are included. I would like to emphasise that these works are or have been widely read, or popular, or influential. Since I have already reviewed works which show Japanese responses to the impact of the continental cultures in Chapter 1, I shall begin with works dating from after the beginning of the western impact.

I have tried to examine Japanese literature that is both old and new in order to find out what the Japanese wrote and expressed. The result shows that defence mechanisms in response to the impact of other cultures are usually not seen overtly. However, a variety of psychological states which reflect the condition for the rise of defence mechanisms are clearly seen.

Specifically, we can identify envy for and admiration of westerners in various literary works published after the turn of the century when the Japanese clearly accepted the superiority of the West. This attitude continued to exist even after the Russo-Japanese War and World War I. The realisation of the unsuccessful identification and rejection by the West are also seen in the form of self-hatred, disappointment, fear of rejection, and making fun of themselves. The feeling that the Japanese are inferior is also expressed.

Among these psychological states, self-hatred and making fun of themselves probably need more explanation. 'Self-hatred' is a concept used in social psychology. This refers to the tendency to dislike or even hate one's own nationality, culture, language, or the self. Making fun of themselves is a common Japanese response when a Japanese is in a state of stress. To smile, to laugh, to joke, or to tease is a method to make oneself feel that the situation one is in is not serious or dangerous. By resorting to behaviour of this kind, one can try to dismiss it. The Japanese love to use this method, as I mentioned earlier, and this response appears over and over in Japanese culture.

After the Meiji Restoration

Before the Meiji Restoration of 1868, there were no significant literary works which interest us in this context. But only a few years after the Meiji Restoration, two relevant works were published. As you will recall, this was the time of *bunmei kaika*, and the Japanese were eager to become westernised. Naturally, the literary works reflected this craze.

In 1871, Kanagaki Robun published *Aguranabe*, which immediately became popular. The story concerns a restaurant which serves beef stew. Because of the *bunmei kaika* craze many Japanese visit the restaurant, and various kinds of guests are described. For example, two girls love beef stew, and one of them reveals that she began to eat beef because she became a concubine of the British Consul, whom she thought was handsome and attractive. The novel implies that those Japanese who do not eat beef are barbarians.

Unlike Kanagaki Robun, Hattori Oga published at least eight literary works which strongly revealed his attitude against westernisation. I am unable to find out to what extent his writings were read by the Japanese, but it is a fact that he was severely criticised by the newspapers for his anti-westernisation view.

Both Kanagaki and Hattori (also called Mantei) wrote in the style and language of the Edo Period, and their works can be classified as novels, essays, funny stories, or criticisms.

Literature After the Russo-Japanese War

The style and language of Japanese literary works began to change sometime after the turn of the century, and several important novelists produced works which are of interest here. Among them, I would like to review the works of Natsume Soseki and Tanizaki Junichiro.

Natsume Soseki (1867-1916)

His novel entitled *Sanshiro*, originally published in 1908, clearly describes the way the Japanese looked at westerners and how they felt about them immediately after the turn of the century. In this novel, a high-school graduate named Sanshiro leaves the southern island of Kyushu and travels by train to Tokyo in order to attend university. On the journey he meets an unusual Japanese and at one of the stations they see several westerners. Sanshiro observes them with great interest and thinks they are beautiful and refined people and he can understand why westerners in Japan are arrogant. He thinks he would feel very inferior if he went to Europe and were surrounded by such people. The conversation between Sanshiro and his travelling companion regarding the westerners went as follows: [my translation]

Man: 'We are miserable. We are weak and we have such faces. Although we won the war against Russia and became a first-rate country, we are no good. Understandably, however, if we look at our buildings or gardens, we can see that they are not much better than our faces...If you have never been to Tokyo, I bet you haven't seen Mount Fuji yet. Look out for it when we get there. That is Japan's number one item to brag about. We have nothing else to brag about. But unfortunately we didn't build Mount Fuji; it is there as a result of natural forces.'
Sanshiro: 'Japan will develop gradually.'
Man: 'I don't agree; we will go downhill.'

In this incident, their understanding that westerners are beautiful and attractive, and their acceptance that Japanese faces are unattractive are clearly stated. As a result, westerners are envied, and their arrogance towards Japanese is accepted.

Later on in the same novel, a Japanese painter appears who reveals his standard of beauty. He paints western-style paintings, and he chooses a Japanese woman who has large, round eyes as his model. He explains that Japanese have small, narrow eyes, but such people are not suitable as models when the western method of painting is employed. He thinks a model with narrow eyes looks like a blind person, and such a woman is unsuitable and ugly as a model.

The woman he chooses as his model also plays the violin, eats sandwiches and is a Catholic. She can speak English and discuss Greek poetry. Sanshiro knows two other women. One is almost entirely Japanese in taste and thinking, and the other is rather more westernised. But Sanshiro likes the woman who poses as a model best, because she is most westernised and up to date.

Here, the painter accepts the western standard of beauty, as he sees it, and rejects the 'almond' eyes of the Japanese. So does Sanshiro. They both prefer a Japanese woman who is more 'western' in facial features. Furthermore, Sanshiro thinks she has an added attraction because she is the most westernised among the three women he knows. She is up to date and desirable.

What we can say about these incidents as a whole is that, by reflecting the times when it was written, the Japanese are described as feeling inferior to westerners both racially and culturally, even after winning the Russo-Japanese War.

Tanizaki Junichiro (1886-1965)

In a work entitled *Ave Maria*, originally published in 1923, Tanizaki deals with a middle-aged writer named Emori in Yokohama. He is in love with a Russian woman named Nina. He knows she is not interested in him, yet he adores her. Emori is sad because he is short. He experiences a 'mysterious fear' because he visualises vast racial differences between them. He says to himself: '...Oh! if the difference between us were only the difference in height!...Does the white mind under that white skin lie somewhere high above me, beyond the reach of the love of the brown mind under this brown skin?'

He daydreams about his affair with her, and in the fantasy, he says; '...I envy you. Japanese can live only within Japan; we are disliked whether we go to America or China...' He fantasises further and says to himself: '...I don't want to see your beautiful white body deteriorate like this in the Japanese streets full of brown faces and brown buildings...Soon...you will have to bury that white body in the ground of the brown country. It saddens me to see that.' He holds her hand in the fantasy and becomes frightened, because he has never done so before on account of the 'shame of leaving brown spots on her white hand' by his bony, ugly fingers. He wishes that she would leave for a place where her 'beautiful fellow mermaids' are.

Tanizaki's idealisation and deification of the western woman is revealed even more when a Japanese woman appears as a heroine. In *Chijin no Ai* ('An Idiot's Love'), published in 1925, he describes a Japanese couple. The man is an engineer named 'Jyoji' and his wife's name is 'Naomi.' It is important to note here that although both names can be Japanese names, they can also be 'George' and 'Naomi,' suggesting identification with western characters in Tanizaki's mind.

The story is narrated by Jyoji. When they meet for the first time, he says: 'This name, "Naomi" is a wonderful name; it's like a westerner...' He thinks her facial features remind him of an American movie actress. He says '[She] certainly looks like a western woman. I know I must be positively biased in the way I look at her...But many people have said the same, so it must be a fact.'

They begin to live together, and they acquire western furniture and keep pictures of western movie actresses on the wall. Since she was a waitress earlier and is uneducated, he decides to make a refined woman out of her. She begins to study western music and English. The objective is to become a refined woman so that she has no need to feel ashamed in the presence of a westerner. They both like to use expressions such as 'even in the presence of a westerner' or 'similar to a westerner.' She says 'How is this? Does my face look like a western face, if I do [contort] like this?' Then they get married.

Jyoji explains why he likes this woman. He thinks that if he had enough money and could do anything he pleased, possibly he might go to Europe, marry a European woman and live there.

But this was not possible for him, so he picked Naomi as his wife because she looks a little 'western' among Japanese.

Thus, Naomi is a substitute for a real western woman, and when he has an opportunity to have the 'honour' of shaking hands with a western woman, he is impressed by the whiteness of her hands. He sees light purple veins under her white skin, and he recognises a difference between her hands and Naomi's hands.

This western woman is his dance teacher, and he dances with her. He constantly worries if his dark face is touching her skin, because his head is at about the same level as her breasts. He says: 'I am fully satisfied merely by looking at that smooth, clean, and beautiful skin at a distance.' Even to shake hands with her is too much for him, and to touch her through that thin dress of hers is an act he must not do. He fears whether he has bad breath or whether his greasy hands are offensive to her.

There are other literary works by Tanizaki, which also present more or less similar psychological responses in the Japanese mind. In his *Aoi Hana* ('Blue Flowers') the heroine also likes to look like a western woman and 'fantasises about becoming a western woman.' In a drama entitled *Honmoku Yawa* ('A Night in Honmoku') a Japanese woman remarks: 'Why are westerners so beautiful? They are so white and attractive. I am so ashamed that I can never come close to them.'

In yet another drama, the attractiveness of and the envy for white skin are combined with an old Japanese folk belief. Traditionally, it was believed that a fox can make fun of people by transforming itself into a human being. In a drama entitled *Byakko no Yu* ('Bathing of a White Fox'), a young man is 'possessed' by a fox, and presumably, earlier, he has become insane after being rejected by a western woman whom he adored. He thinks this woman takes a bath at a spa every night but in reality, she is a transformed fox to deceive him. He is infatuated with her blond hair and white skin. Finally, he is carried away by three foxes and later found dead in a stream.

In these works by Tanizaki, the way the Japanese responded to the West is clearly shown. In *Chijin no Ai*, identification is shown by having a couple named 'Jyoji' and 'Naomi.' They try to give a western look to the interior of their home. He is happy to know that his wife looks like a western woman, which is exactly why he chose to marry her. For her part, she, too, tries to look like a western woman. This is also true for the woman in *Aoi Hana*, who fantasises about being a western woman. Naomi in *Chijin no Ai* tries to look and behave like a western woman so that she will not feel ashamed in the presence of a westerner.

But in the final analysis, Naomi is only a substitute for a real western woman, and Jyoji is shocked when he realises the differences between Naomi and a Caucasian woman. He is disappointed to say the least. Since identification with westerners is already in the minds of these Japanese, to be forced to recognise the racial differences makes them feel inferior, and they envy and admire westerners. Jyoji feels inferior to his dance teacher, as does a woman in *Honmoku Yawa*. The Caucasian racial traits are idealised, admired, and envied. In *Byakko no Yu* the same Japanese response is presented by a transformed fox with a white skin and blond hair.

The same motif is described also in *Ave Maria*. The Japanese man, Emori, feels a vast distance between him and the Russian woman, Nina, and because of this distance based on the racial differences, he adores and deifies her. He assumes that she belongs to a superior race and believes that a person of a superior race should not live among a people of an inferior race, such as his. This psychology goes on to develop into 'self-hatred.' He is afraid of leaving brown spots on her when he holds her hands in a fantasy. The Japanese are described as a brown people, and they are not good for her because after all, she is a beautiful mermaid just like the others of her kind.

By reflecting the time of strong anti-Japanese feelings in Europe and America, the Japanese described by Tanizaki are afraid of being rejected. Emori says: '...we are disliked whether we go to America or China...' and Jyoji is afraid that he may be offensive to his dance teacher. This pessimistic feeling is most symbolically presented in *Byakko no Yu*, in which the young insane Japanese is killed by three foxes, suggesting that the identification with the West is tragic and can never be successful.

Other Authors

I reviewed some of the works by Natsume Soseki and Tanizaki Junichiro because these works clearly show the psychology of the Japanese in response to western rejection, and also because both authors are very important and influential in Japanese literature in the twentieth century. The fact that they are among the most important figures in contemporary Japanese literature is sufficient to convince you, I think, that Japanese readers understood and appreciated their writing. That in turn suggests that many Japanese thought and felt like the Japanese portrayed in these stories.

It is not difficult to come across brief statements of a similar nature in the works of novelists who are recognised as first-rate authors in Japan. For example, Nagai Kafu writes as follows in his *Amerika Monogatari* ('Tales from America'). 'I am one of those who admire the physical beauty of the western woman...I am one of those who would like to show an unlimited respect for them...In contrast, Japanese women totally lack the ability [to be beautiful].' In a similar work entitled *Furansu Monogatari* ('Tales from France'), he describes a hero, who presumably is Nagai himself and hates Japanese 'to such an extent and he cannot really understand why.' These works were published in 1908 and 1909.

Another novelist, who was once considered for a Nobel Prize in literature may be added as well. Serizawa Kojiro published *Pari ni Shisu* ('To die in Paris') in 1942. At the beginning of this novel, the hero describes what he feels. He says: 'Japan has absorbed the culture of the West well enough and now there are Japanese women who are not inferior in front of western women when they are judged by the western standard of beauty. Miss Mariko is like a western woman not only in her facial features, but also in her thoughts and feelings...'

In the same novel, a woman tells the reader how she felt when she met a Japanese woman who was married to an Englishman. She states: 'She dressed well in western clothes, and she walked just like a western woman. Since this is the first time for me to wear a western dress, I secretly tried to imitate her way of walking...I looked at her with envy and hoped that some day I would be able to walk like western women without being ashamed.'

Of course, in addition to this type of so-called high-brow literature for intellectuals, there is the popular fiction for the masses. Among the popular authors I would like to mention Tani Jyoji here. He lived in the United States for a while as an immigrant and experienced American anti-Japanese attitudes at first hand. Later he returned to Japan and became immensely successful as an author with three different pen names. In a work entitled *Tekisasu Mushuku* ('A Texas Tramp'), he describes a Japanese who fights, cheats, and lives wildly in America without allowing himself to be subjected to the discrimination of the 1920s.

There were also popular writers for young people whose books reflected the climate of the period in one way or another. For example, the topics covered by Oshikawa Shunro included anti-Japanese attitudes in the West and Japanese reaction, excellence of the Japanese spirit, the future racial war, Japan as a strong military power, the unification of Asia against the West, and Japan's efforts to make the Philippines an independent nation. His books were enthusiastically read by youngsters in the early part of the twentieth century. His works became popular again, perhaps because of the themes he treated towards the end of World War II.

Literature After World War II

Literary activities in Japan during World War II were completely controlled by the military. The writers were forced to cooperate with the military government, and those who refused were persecuted in both visible and invisible ways. As a result, chauvinistic and racist literature appeared. However, none of these works has ever been considered a first-rate literary work. Indeed, practically all of them have been entirely forgotten since the war.

When it became widely known by the Japanese that the official policy of the occupation forces was to change Japan in the direction of western democracy, Japanese literature once again began to show the same psychological responses.

Endo Shusaku (1923-)

In his *Ryugaku* ('Study Abroad'), published in 1965, Endo describes a Japanese lecturer in French who goes to France. He experiences a series of shocks, discouragements, disillusions, and disappointments because of the racial and cultural differences between France and Japan. At Hamburg International Airport, Tanaka, the lecturer, recognises Japanese passengers even in the dark because 'they talk very loud without paying attention to where they are.' In a restaurant at the airport, a group of Japanese passengers see another Japanese sitting alone in the same restaurant. One of them suggests he should be invited to the same table, but another man in the group says the stranger avoided eye contact and ignored him in the airplane.

Endo writes: 'He seems to have noticed that he is being watched. Wearing thick glasses, he stiffened his face, and upon eye contact, he at once avoided it precisely as he did before and turned his head to a painting on the wall. Even though he is a Japanese, his attitude is that he belongs to a race different from yours.'

In a subway train, Tanaka also sees a Japanese, but this man, too, avoids eye contact and pretends to watch the scenery outside the window. He seems to be afraid of being spoken to in Japanese when he is in France. Tanaka also meets a Japanese who came to France as an employee of the Bank of Japan, but because he married a French woman, he lost his job. He is unhappy because he is only half Japanese, and yet he cannot be French.

When Tanaka was teaching in Japan, he only heard about the success stories of his colleagues who had been to France before, and for the first time, he experiences miserable feelings and insulting treatments by being in France.

In this novel, as in the case of Tanizaki's works, the hero identifies with westerners relatively unconsciously before having extensive contact with them. But after being in France, both racial and cultural differences are so overwhelming that the hero experiences an intense shock. He realises that his identification has been very incomplete and unsatisfactory. This is mostly expressed through his sense of rejection by the French and French culture.

Endo also consistently describes the phenomenon of 'self-hatred.' The Japanese who talk loud at Hamburg Airport are offensive and disliked by the hero. The avoidance of eye contact is also an expression of self-hatred, in the sense that one rejects contact with someone of the same racial or ethnic background. One rejects one's own group because one identifies oneself with a group 'better' than one's own group. If that group rejects one's own group, one must also do so as a result of identification.

Another work by Endo is entitled *Aden Made* ('Up to Aden'), published in 1954. This story concerns a Japanese student in France and his French girl-friend. He is uncertain if she really accepts him, and when they kiss each other for the first time, he questions her: 'Is this all right? Are you sure?' When they show their naked bodies to each other, he is forced to see vast racial differences in the colours of their bodies and hair. He suffers from an intense feeling of racial inferiority. His body is unlively and of a dull, dark, and yellow colour. He can see neither beauty nor harmony when his body and hers are together. He thinks the combination is very ugly. He feels as if he were a yellow worm on a white petal. The yellow colour reminds him of human excrement. He wants to cover both his face and body by his hands, and he turns off the light in order to make his body invisible.

After this incident, his sense of equality disappears and he accepts that he belongs to an inferior race. He experiences some pleasure through being treated sadistically by her during intercourse. He explains that he wants to insult himself because he is yellow and therefore inferior. He also thinks that black is an ugly skin colour. It is a 'sinful' colour. But a dark yellow colour is even more miserable than black.

When he first came to Europe three years ago, he did not think much about his skin colour. At that time, the Japanese were just like Europeans, having the same rationality and concepts. But now after three years in Europe and on his way home to Japan, he thinks he is yellow for ever, and she is white for ever.

This novel begins with a relatively unconscious identification on the part of the Japanese student before he came to France. He used to think that the Japanese were just like Europeans. But when he is actually exposed to the situation in which he kisses a French woman, he realises that he is afraid of being rejected. When he sees her naked body along with his own, his recognition of the vast racial differences between them makes him envy her race, which he admires. He completely accepts the racial value judgement of the West, and this leads him to think that both black and yellow skins are ugly. Because of this identification, he experiences self-hatred, and he gets pleasure from being treated sadistically by her. On his way back to Japan, he feels intensely the vast distance between himself and the West.

Numa Shozo (? -?)

The true identity of this author is unknown. He is remembered for his science fiction novel entitled *Kachikujin Yapu* ('The *Yapu:* The Domesticated People'), published in a magazine between 1957 and 1959 — a work which was highly acclaimed by the internationally known author, Mishima Yukio. The novel was later published as a book, which became popular among young people and sold well.

According to Numa's story, World War III breaks out in 1978, and most of the people on earth perish. England has developed its own space ship secretly, and Princess Margaret and 1,000 young men emigrate to another planet. After the war, weird surviving creatures are discovered in Japan, and they look somewhat like gorillas or ape men. They are captured and shipped to the new colonising planet.

These creatures are not considered as human beings. They are domesticated animals. They are the descendants of the Japanese and are called *yapu*. *Yapu* are surgically operated on immediately after birth and they are physically modified, so that the people of the new colony can use them as furniture, toilets, handbags, conveyances, and so on.

This is a most weird and bizarre science fiction story describing as it does the ways *yapu* are mutilated and treated as moving living objects. Furthermore, in this story, psychological responses such as envy, admiration, self-hatred, fear of rejection, feeling of inferiority, and disappointment, which are found in most of the works reviewed above are absent. Instead, the consistent and only motif is to make fun of the *yapu*, the descendants of the Japanese. These creatures are modified and controlled to such an extent by means of advanced medical technology and engineering that there is no room for them to feel inferior or envious. It appears that the author's intention is to make fun of the Japanese.

This attitude can be considered a form of reaction formation, in the sense that smiles, laughter, and joking are expressions of reaction formation. To deal with an unpleasant situation or a danger by these methods is to try to convince oneself that it is not at all unpleasant or dangerous. Rather, it becomes something funny or amusing instead. An unpleasant fact is turned into a pleasant fact. A danger is turned into an amusement. Western rejection becomes an entertainment in this science fiction story and in this sense, it is typically Japanese.

Other Authors

Japanese literature after the war is full of psychological responses which covertly or overtly show envy and admiration of westerners and a realisation of unsuccessful identification. These responses are unlikely to be handled as the main theme of a novel in most cases, but are sometimes casually included. However, from the standpoint of understanding Japanese culture, I think these casual descriptions are equally valuable.

It is not really feasible here to give multiple examples but I would like to mention two authors in particular. In 1962 Oda Makoto published a novel entitled *Amerika*. The hero is a Japanese business student studying in the United States. He has an American girl-friend. When a Mexican man asks him if she is his wife, he reveals his psychology clearly:

'Are you a married couple?' whispered the young man suddenly.

'You...?'

'Yes, you and that American lady.'

I nodded.

'I envy you.'

I thought he was sarcastic. But he was serious. I asked him deliberately.

'What?'

The young man blushed and said.

'...Because you are married to an American woman.'

'Why?'

The young man did not answer. Perhaps he could not answer. I suddenly felt a sadistic pleasure. No, it might be better to call it a sense of superiority.

He experiences 'an offensive but ecstatic pleasure' when his girl-friend says that his skin is 'as white as' hers. In the south, he uses facilities for 'whites only' without hesitation and without any problem. But he gradually becomes uncertain about his identity, and finally he participates in the civil rights movement and sits down.

In this novel, then, like many other novels of a similar nature, the hero shows unconscious identification with Caucasians, and finds it pleasurable when his identification turns out to be successful. The value of this work as a novel, however, lies in the fact that the hero discovers something about his identity by experiencing life in the United States.

. Ito Sei is the other novelist I would like to mention here. He completed his novel entitled *Hi no Tori* ('The Firebird') in 1953. This novel describes an actress whose father is British. She is narcissistic because her skin is completely white without any pigment, and also because she has dark blue or green eyes and reddish dark hair.

But as she gets older, she realises that her face is a mongoloid face, resembling her mother and sister. She becomes frightened. She tries to convince herself that as an actress, she can remain beautiful by the use of good make-up. Although this is not the theme of the novel, these descriptions nevertheless do show quite well on the one hand envy and admiration of Caucasian racial traits and self-hatred on the other.

10 Popular Culture in Japan

EVEN THOUGH the way it expresses itself may not always be very artistic or refined, popular culture shows what a particular people like, enjoy, and think. In this sense, to study the popular culture of Japan is another way of understanding the Japanese.

The western impact on Japanese popular culture began to be seen immediately after the Meiji Restoration of 1868. That was the time of *bunmei kaika;* or the new era of 'getting civilised.' Several songs describing this new craze became 'top of the pops.' Some were simply descriptive, recounting what was meant by *bunmei kaika;* others were a bit sarcastic, describing what confusing times they were and how difficult it was for the masses to understand what was going on. It appears that the masses felt a significant psychological distance to western cultures, and the songs in essence summed up their reactions.

After the turn of the century, and probably after the first decade in the twentieth century, the masses became more sensitive and responsive to things western. This took place along with the development of modern capitalism and the emergence of the modern, white-collar Japanese middle class.

The expression, *haikara,* began to be used widely in Japanese society, and the new white-collar middle class wanted to be *haikara.* This adjective describes any condition which is up to date, attractive, fashionable, and nice, and this meant imitation of things western. To be *haikara* was to wear western clothes, to wear western shoes, to eat western foods, to follow western customs, and to think and behave like a westerner. Another expression *yokogaeri* meant someone who had come back from Europe or America, and such a person acquired great prestige. A *yokogaeri* was most likely to show off his or her experience abroad by being *haikara*, while others who were not *yokogaeri* admired and envied such a person. But by imitating a *yokagaeri*, they, too, could be *haikara*.

Later another expression, *modan*, began to be used. This comes from the English word 'modern,' and as in the case of *haikara*, this adjective was used to refer to a westernised Japanese. A westernised man was a *mobo* (modern boy) while a westernised woman was a *moga* (modern girl). The Japanese who were *haikara* or *modan* were well described in novels in the early twentieth century by many novelists, including Natsume Soseki and Tanizaki Junichiro, as we have seen.

Despite the rise of anti-western political ideology and the development of expansionism and colonialism in the 1920s and 1930s, the popular culture in Japan consistently showed the same characteristic. It was nice and attractive and desirable to be *haikara* and *modan*. Political ideology or international relations could hardly change the general trend of popular culture.

During World War II, the military government decided that western influences on Japanese culture were unacceptable and tried to get rid of them. For example, borrowed English or French words were outlawed. The cultures of the Axis countries, however, were not included; German music or literature, for example, remained perfectly acceptable.

Through the censored and controlled mass media, the official version of what constituted a desirable and attractive Japanese was fed to the masses. The ideal Japanese man, for example, was one who was prepared to serve and die for the Emperor, and the ideal Japanese woman was the mother who willingly offered her son as a soldier and rejoiced upon learning that he had been killed in battle, because that was a contribution to the Divine Land and the Emperor. Indeed, a Japanese soldier was supposed to shout, *Tenno Heika Banzai!* (Long Live the Emperor!) when he knew he was going to die from a battle wound. Schoolboys were encouraged to study hard, so that they would be admitted to the prestigious Navy Academy. Towards the end of the war, they were encouraged to become *kamikaze* pilots.

To some extent, as a totalitarian country during the war, Japan was in a position to halt the trend of more and more westernisation at the visible, official level, because the military government could simply forbid and punish any pro-western ideology or behaviour by means of, for example, the secret police (*Tokko Keisatsu*). But that does not mean the government could effectively change the direction of the post-Meiji Restoration trends.

Indeed, soon after the beginning of the Occupation, the same characteristics of Japanese popular culture before the war became clearly visible. For example, Japan's first best-seller after the war was an English-Japanese conversation handbook, which sold more than 360,000 copies. In 1949, there were about 2,000 schools teaching 200,000 Japanese women how to sew American dresses. According to an opinion survey conducted in 1951, 46.9% of the respondents answered that the Japanese were inferior to the Americans and the British, and only 22.9% of the respondents answered that the Japanese were not inferior to them. Although the Japanese began to show a more positive image of themselves later, especially after the period of rapid economic growth, the basic characteristic of their popular culture remains the same as ever.

Physical Identification and Popular Culture

When Japanese identify with westerners, the problem of physical differences emerges. After all, most Japanese do not look like most westerners. As we have already seen, the Japanese have been forced to recognise this problem in two ways. First, they were rejected and discriminated against when they acted like a western, colonising people. The finger of accusation was pointed at them and they were attacked in racial terms — at least they thought they were — in matters relating to international trade, diplomacy, and emigration.

Second, even for the Japanese, it was not easy to believe that they had succeeded completely in becoming like westerners because of the way they looked. This problem of physical differences between westerners and Japanese was dealt with partly by means of reaction formation by claiming the 'racial superiority' of the Japanese until the end of World War II. But since this resulted in a catastrophic disaster, they are no longer able to resort to this defence mechanism.

Since World War II, the Japanese have been faced with two basic options in the way they deal with the problem of physical differences when they identify with westerners. First, even though they may never be exactly the same as westerners in appearance, the Japanese nevertheless set the standard of the ideal human being and beauty by accepting the physical characteristics of westerners. They then try hard to reduce the differences between themselves and westerners by a variety of means. This is the same approach used by some Afro-Americans.

Second, another way to deal with this disturbing problem is to accept the differences more or less reluctantly and to make fun of themselves. This is a form of reaction formation, in the sense that to laugh at the problem one has is to consider it insignificant, amusing, or pleasant.

I hope you will allow me to emphasise this point once again here as a typical Japanese response. A *samurai* smiled when he committed *seppuku,* and a *kamikaze* pilot also smiled before leaving for the suicide mission. In present-day Japan, a teenage girl smiles and giggles when spoken to by a westerner.

The reason why I am returning to this form of reaction formation is that often a Japanese smile or laughter is puzzling or even offensive to some westerners. For example, the *Atlantic Monthly* published an annoyed reaction of an American in Japan in its April 1946 issue as follows: '[Japanese] asked me if their balloon bomb had done any damage in the States. I replied that as far as I knew, they had done no damage and were not worth a damn. Everybody around us laughed heartily; evidently I had said something very funny.'

Both methods of dealing with the problem of racial differences, namely, (1) to try to resemble westerners as much as possible, and (2) to make fun of themselves, are significant sources of contemporary Japanese popular culture. When the first approach is chosen and the physical characteristics of westerners are considered the standards of beauty, commercialism takes over. The cosmetic industry advertises products which claim to make Japanese women as beautiful as western women. Eye shadows are emphasised, presumably because this form of make-up allows oriental eyes to appear more deeply set than they actually are. Hair is also bleached to make it red or brown or even blond.

When Japanese realise that sun-tan lotions are sold in western countries in order to make the skin brown, they also buy such products — despite the fact that, in general, they already have a natural tan! It is conceivable, I suppose, that to get tanned and to become brown suggest that there is enough scope for the skin to get darker; such 'logical' thinking, it would appear, is sufficiently satisfying to the Japanese mind.

For some, once they have realised that their eyes are significantly different from westerners' eyes, they often try to hide their eyes by wearing sun-glasses. This can be inferred from the fact that some Japanese use sun glasses when they do not need them — for example, at night or in winter when there is no snow around. They also like to wear sun glasses when they travel abroad. For these Japanese, the eyes are defective parts of their bodies merely because they are different from Caucasian eyes.

Some Japanese go to the expense of cosmetic surgery to achieve the same objective. Typically, the nose is heightened, the epicanthic folds (which make the oriental eyes 'almond-like') are removed, and the folds over both eyes are raised in order to make the eyes less slit-like. It is a thriving and highly profitable business. On 1 October 1985 the *Japan Times* stated that many co-eds undergo cosmetic surgery before they go job-hunting. Most of them make their eyelids double or make their noses higher. According to the newspaper, it costs about 150,000 yen for an operation on the eyes and about 200,000 yen for a nose job. Many Japanese women also wish to reduce their high cheek bones and protruding teeth; both are rather common oriental characteristics.

According to Japanese values, in earlier times, mutilation of the body was considered highly objectionable. For example, eunuchs were commonplace in China and Korea but the Japanese never adopted this custom. For the same reason, at least in historic Japan, ear-piercing was never practised. But now many Japanese women from all walks of life get their ears pierced, simply because it is customary for western women to do it.

In the mass media, Caucasians and part-Caucasians appear extensively in TV commercials and posters as well as advertisements in magazines and newspapers. Some of them are highly paid and well-known actors, actresses, singers, professional athletes, or entertainers in Europe or America. Furthermore, they advertise Japanese products. The rationale is that a well-known western celebrity has considerable powers of persuasion when he or she is seen to endorse a particular product. The fact is, the technique is very successful for selling goods and services. There are many well-known cases in which sales increased phenomenally merely because a western celebrity was used in the advertisement.

Models at Japanese fashion shows are quite often Caucasians, and when Japanese appear as models, it is those Japanese who are considered to be closest to western standards of beauty. This would also explain why the mannequins in Japanese stores are almost always western in physical features, and why they model not only the latest fashions from London, Paris, Milan and New York, but also traditional Japanese *kimono*.

Even official publications, brochures, and manuals published by the government or the municipalities quite often show drawings of people with red or brown hair even though these publications are written entirely in Japanese and readers are almost totally Japanese. It goes without saying that the Japanese are delighted to learn that they are treated as 'honorary whites' in South Africa.

At the same time, dark-skinned Japanese show an ambivalent attitude towards light-skinned Japanese. If a light-skinned person is obviously western, a dark-skinned Japanese can easily accept the fact. But if the light-skinned person is otherwise Japanese, an ambivalent attitude follows. In essence, such a person is envied for two reasons. First, a light skin is a western characteristic, and it is therefore envied. Second, a light skin has been traditionally valued in Japan even before the extensive contact with the West. With this background, reaction formation can be more easily practised on the light-skinned Japanese. For example, a light-skinned Japanese man is more likely to be ridiculed and laughed at by a dark-skinned Japanese, who might say: 'You look very pale. Are you sick?' or 'When did you get out of the hospital?' Here, 'I envy you because you have a light skin' is turned into 'I feel sorry for you because you have a light skin and that is not healthy.'

Such situations are a disguised form of self-hatred, because a dark-skinned Japanese envies light-skinned Japanese, which in turn means that he dislikes his own dark skin. Since he cannot change his skin colour, he must somehow defend his position in relation to light-skinned Japanese. Reaction formation is used, and he ridicules light-skinned Japanese as a result.

Self-hatred directed against the Japanese as an ethnic group is well known among the Japanese themselves. We have already seen what happens when a Japanese sees another Japanese in a foreign country; they both tend to avoid each other, and sometimes they show open hostility towards each other. For example, according to two Japanese who have had extensive experience as guides for Japanese tourists abroad, this phenomenon is commonplace. They write: 'Regrettably, we Japanese seem to avoid eye contact and even refuse to go near other Japanese when we meet in the street [in a foreign country],' while another remarks that 'Japanese pretend that they do not recognise each other even when they see each other.' Japanese novels often describe self-hatred, examples of which were given in the preceding chapter.

Expressions of Physical Desirability

The two methods used to deal with the problem of racial differences are reflected in the language spoken in contemporary Japan. There are many common expressions which suggest the desirability of Caucasian physical features (see Table 1, p. 152).

I should add that when these expressions are used among the Japanese, even when there are no explicit implications in racial terms, Caucasian standards are meant in most cases. For example *gaijin* literally means a 'person from outside,' namely 'foreigner,' but this almost always means a westerner. To be 'unlike a Japanese' signifies to be like a foreigner, and that means 'Caucasian.' To describe a Japanese in this manner is a compliment to him or her. To be 'similar to a foreigner' means to be similar to a westerner, and this too, is a compliment. When such expressions are used to describe facial features, the implication is that the face is similar to a western face, and this is also a compliment.

You will appreciate that all of these expressions dealing with facial features highlight certain characteristics which are usually lacking or less common in a Japanese face. Thus, by Japanese standards of beauty a well-shaped nose is more desirable than a flat nose, and large, round eyes are more desirable than narrow, slit-like 'almond' eyes. Similarly, a 'deeply curved' face with a well-shaped conspicuous nose and deeply set eyes are more desirable than a round, flat face.

A Japanese who can satisfy these requirements is approved and considered *sumato* ('smart'), *fasshonaburu* ('fashionable'), or *kakkoii*. Quite often the hero or heroine in a contemporary Japanese novel is such a person. One example is the hero in Oda's novel *Amerika*, which I mentioned earlier. The same

/es may be used in order to describe a person who has
esternised satisfactorily.

Despite the striving for western standards of handsomeness
and beauty, many Japanese are far from having these desired
characteristics. As a result, a large number of expressions have
been made up in order to laugh at oneself and other Japanese
who are in their eyes ugly (see Table 2, p. 152).

These expressions are used for describing a Japanese who is
very dissimilar to a westerner. The Japanese seem to be especially
sensitive about short legs. Unfortunately, certain ethnic groups
are referred to in these expressions, and we may consider this as
a form of projection; the Japanese may be trying to deal with
the problem of being different from Caucasians by projecting
their own traits which they dislike onto another ethnic group.

This aspect of Japanese popular culture is consistently found
in the world of entertainment. Comedians, *manzai* (two
comedians who always work in a pair and tell funny stories and
jokes), and *rakugoka* (a traditional entertainer, teller of jokes and
funny stories) almost routinely consider that to make people
laugh by ridiculing other people is a proper way to entertain.
When this method is exploited in a comedy, often a person of
a rural background speaking a dialect with many unattractive
and ugly physical features appears; such a person may be a young
girl.

Quite often when a *manzai* pair appears on stage, one of
them insults the partner by pointing out his or her unattractive
and ugly physical features and then laughs; then the partner who
has been ridiculed counterattacks by pointing out the detractor's
unattractive and ugly features. This may involve a part of the
body which has nothing to do with racial differences such as
obesity or baldness. In fact, it is common in Japanese culture as
a whole to laugh at people by pointing out unattractive physical
features. This has no particular relationship with the level of
education or occupation or income. I have seen many university
professors who talk like *manzai*.

The Japanese have certain stereotyped ideas about the
physical characteristics of westerners, and these ideas are shown
in their popular culture. When a westerner is drawn in a cartoon,
he or she has a huge, pointed nose and is very large, compared
with a Japanese in the same cartoon. When a western woman
is drawn, she is likely to have a huge bust — showing the artist

has implicitly accepted the western idea of an attractive woman through exaggeration. At the same time, these drawings project the Japanese ideal in men and women.

Results of Identification in Popular Culture

Popular culture in present-day Japan also shows identification with westerners in a variety of forms without directly involving attempts to identify physically. The youth culture of any country invariably follows fads (usually set elsewhere). Japan is no exception. Japanese youths, for example, are quick to follow American college fads and fashions, in the wearing of blue jeans, college sweat shirts (of American colleges, of course), T-shirts, bags, shoes, long hair, and styles of moustache and beard.

An old fad which is still part of current culture among Japanese college kids is the use of ex-US military items, such as bags and uniforms. This phenomenon is strikingly similar to the prisoners' behaviour in the Nazi concentration camp (see Appendix), where some prisoners greatly valued old pieces of Gestapo uniforms and even tried to alter their own clothes to resemble Nazi uniforms. In fact, it is interesting to note that fake American military uniforms are produced and sold locally in Japan. If you cannot get the envied item which the aggressor has, one solution is to imitate it. The closer the imitation, the better.

This would explain why the Japanese produced so many copy-cat products in the past. It is widely known that many of these items were exported. There were Japanese watches, for example, which looked exactly like the world-renowned Swiss makes, and there were many Japanese-made cameras which were perfect replicas of the Leica cameras. In the past, a Swiss watch or a Leica was a prestige item in Japan, because such an item was a product of the West and was also very expensive. Most Japanese could not afford these luxuries, and copy-cat products could meet the Japanese demands in two ways. A genuine Swiss watch or a Leica enhanced the Japanese owner's prestige because it came from the peoples the Japanese identified with, making them *haikara* and *modan*. So, since most Japanese at the time could not afford the real thing, one solution was to obtain a cheaper copy-cat substitute.

I do not think for a minute the Japanese felt that the 'replica' industry was unethical or involved any sense of guilt whatsoever.

Such behaviour after all, has been a part of Japanese culture for centuries. In the past, Japanese identified with the peoples on the continent, and by imitating them, they built up their own culture. As far as the Japanese are concerned, to copy is to live.

TV in Japan, like the rest of the industrialised world today, is undoubtedly the most influential medium of mass communication, and identification with the West, especially American culture, is consistently seen on TV. For example, if a Japanese soap opera involves a romance between a westerner and a Japanese, the viewers' response is invariably favourable. There is also a clear tendency to get westerners to appear on TV and offer their comments and opinions on 'things Japanese,' such as customs, mishaps, accidents, political scandals, educational systems, and almost anything that is a topical issue of debate.

When TV stations televise old festivals and ceremonies in various parts of Japan, as a matter of routine, they also feature the reactions of any western tourists who might be watching the events as part of the crowd. In the world of *sumo* (Japanese wrestling), there used to be a famous Hawaiian-born, naturalised *sumo* wrestler; when he appeared in the ring, westerners among the spectators were consistently shown on the TV screen and their reactions were broadcast all over Japan.

In these situations, western opinions are used in order to find out whether or not the Japanese are behaving properly. The Japanese government regularly conducts opinion surveys in the West, in order to find out what the West thinks about Japan. This is exactly the psychology of Naomi in Tanizaki's novel, 'An Idiot's Love,' who consistently keeps asking her husband and herself if she is doing all right and should not feel ashamed in the presence of a westerner.

This strong tendency to seek western opinions and reactions explains why westerners consistently appear in TV commercials even when the products to be sold are entirely Japanese. A westerner's opinion is a persuading force. Japanese are led to buy the products approved by westerners because if westerners like the products, Japanese, too, must like them as a result of identification.

Western customs such as Christmas and St Valentine's Day are similarly exploited commercially even though Christians in Japan are numerically very insignificant. Merely because westerners give presents on such occasions, Japanese are persuaded by department stores that they, too, must buy gifts. Similarly, non-Christian Japanese like to get married in a church because westerners do. The distortion of western culture is so much more obvious when Japanese couples go on a honeymoon trip abroad *in a group*, as part of a huge group of newly-weds!

Advertisements are typically full of English words and Japanese expressions which are made up by using English words. Trade names especially carry English or English-sounding names. Sometimes such names are direct imitations of similar-sounding western trade names.

For example, a man named Ishibashi, which means 'stone bridge' in English, started a tyre-manufacturing company, and used the trade name 'Bridgestone,' by reversing his name and imitating the American trade name 'Firestone.' A trade name may be made up by adding an English word to a Japanese word so that the whole trade name sounds like an English word. Sometime ago, there was a Japanese-made car called *Datto*, which roughly translated means 'rapidly running rabbit.' Later, when a new model was launched it was named 'Datsun.' The word 'sun' here was derived from the English word 'son,' because the new car belonged to the next generation. Thus, 'Datsun' means the 'son' of *Datto*.

Even when Japanese words are used as a trade name, it is often arranged in such a way that the result sounds like an English word. For example, three brothers started a whisky company by copying the know-how of Scotch whisky production. The Japanese word for three is *san*, and since there were three men named 'Torii,' the trade name became 'Suntory,' spelling it as if it were an English word.

The prestige attached to English or English-sounding expressions seems to be effective in influencing people not only for making people buy commercial products, but also for making people vote, changing opinions, or impressing people. Politicians like to use English words in political speeches, but often they dig up very rare or obsolete words from a dictionary so that what they are saying is unintelligible or meaningless even to a native speaker of English. They also make up new expressions by combining English words, but these expressions are not used in English-speaking countries and again they are unintelligible or meaningless. The fact that such expressions could end up as gobbledygook (as they often do) or with awkward or funny implications means nothing to the Japanese. They simply feel something very important has been expressed, and that serves the purpose. It could be said that the language spoken in present-day Japan is becoming more and more like Pidgin English, albeit a different variety. Pidgin English is spoken even now in Melanesia.

To talk like this is an important way to impress people, which is a prerequisite for being considered an intellectual. As a result, there are innumerable language schools all over Japan — most of them teaching English to middle-class white-collar workers (sometimes involving contracts to send teachers to a company's offices). Whether or not the 'students' actually learn English is another matter. All they have to do is to pick up some English words and expressions, so that they can show off their knowledge of English whenever an opportunity arises.

I might add that even in a situation like this, a disguised form of self-hatred is sometimes apparent. There are cases of Japanese Americans with good qualifications and experience in teaching English as a foreign language who have been discriminated against when seeking teaching posts at such language schools, merely because they are not Caucasians. Caucasians are preferred as teachers of English, even when they are less qualified or even when their native tongue is not English. The language schools explain the reason by saying that Japanese prefer Caucasians as their teachers.[1]

Singers, actors, actresses, entertainers, writers and others who have to promote themselves commercially also use western names. However, they usually keep their Japanese family names. There are two possible reasons for this. First, a combination of a Japanese family name and a western first name suggests that such a person is a national of a western country with Japanese ancestry such as a Japanese American. This reflects the same desire to be Japanese Americans expressed by two teenage robbers mentioned in Chapter 8. When a Japanese cannot pass for a Caucasian, to try to pass for a Japanese American or some kind of a hyphenated westerner is ultimately the only realistic solution available — in addition, of course, to extensive cosmetic surgery. Second, social psychologists tell us that any unusual combination is more likely to attract attention than a more common combination. In this sense, combining a Japanese and a western name may be more effective in selling oneself in the commercial world than having a completely Japanese name.

Another common method for these 'high profile' people is to take the name of a well-known western actor, actress, writer, and so on and to pronounce it in the Japanese way. This then becomes the person's 'trade name' which when pronounced, sounds like a Japanese name, but at the same time, Japanese realise that the name has been derived from a well-known western personality. A few examples are Edogawa Ranpo (Edgar Allan Poe), Masuda Kiton (Buster Keaton), and Tani Kei (Danny Kaye).

An interesting consequence of identification with westerners is that, if westerners evaluate a certain thing differently from the Japanese, they begin to change their evaluation towards the western viewpoint. For example, traditionally, the Japanese rejected a dark skin, and consequently rejected Africans and Afro-Americans. However, although this attitude still exists, it is probably correct to say that sometime after the beginning of the civil rights movement in the United States (1960s), the Japanese began to be a little less prejudiced towards Africans and Afro-Americans. This is because the Europeans and the majority of Americans became less prejudiced towards them — at least as far as official policies are concerned.

Similarly, as a result of identification, things which are not appreciated by the West are not good in the eyes of the Japanese. As a result, if such things are found in the Japan, the Japanese tend to feel a sense of shame. For example, when it is discovered that westerners think it objectionable to make a noise when one eats, and also that most Japanese eat that way, they feel ashamed. Handbooks and guidebooks on foreign travel usually have a chapter on eating, which warns Japanese not to make a noise when they eat. Many Japanese are also ashamed to have an 'arranged' marriage, and according to one study, those who had acquired arranged mates responded that they would like to have a 'love match' if they could get married again. As regards sexual behaviour, increasingly Japanese youths imitate American youths.

To follow the western way of thinking sometimes produces the most unexpected results. Consider, for example, the fact that in Japan, people of Jewish background, no matter how this may be defined, are virtually non-existent. Yet it is possible to come across negative expressions about the Jews. Although, fortunately

not widely known, one example is the use of the term *kyu-ichi*.
In Japanese *kyu* means nine, and *ichi* means one. If nine is added
to one, ten is obtained, and the Japanese word for ten is *jyu*,
which sounds similar to the English word 'Jew.' In itself the
expression is not particularly derogatory, but at the same time,
it is not favourable either; rather, it conveys a negative
impression. The fact that most Japanese know almost nothing
about Jewish characteristics, Jewish history or customs, or Judaism
itself does not make any difference. The fact that some westerners
still maintain a negative attitude towards them is enough to make
some Japanese think the same way.

11 *Whither Japan?*

IN THIS BOOK, I have tried to look at Japanese culture from a psychoanalytic point of view. A total of nine defence mechanism concepts have been applied and of these the most important is undoubtedly identification with the aggressor. This is because the Japanese have been aware of more advanced and powerful peoples throughout much of their history. The impact of the West on Japan from the middle of the nineteenth century and Japan's defeat in World War II were of decisive importance in motivating the Japanese to resort to identification with the aggressor.

The Background of Economic Growth

Generally speaking, after her defeat in World War II Japan was psychoanalytically very similar to the Japan after the Meiji Restoration of 1868. In both situations, the Japanese were forced to understand clearly that they had suffered insults precisely because their science and technology were inferior to those of the aggressors. In 1868, the Japanese knew that they had been forced to open the country and to accept various unjust treaties against their will because the western military was indisputably superior to theirs. In 1945, the Japanese knew that they were defeated because the Allies had more advanced weapons such as A-bombs. Consequently, in both situations, the Japanese realised fully that the power of science and technology was truly a matter of life or death. No wonder, therefore that they identified with the aggressor.

However, there is an important difference between the two. After the Meiji Restoration, the Japanese were eager to modernise and build up their military in order to fight back. But Japan after World War II was very different. The effects of the two A-bombs both physically and psychologically were so extensive and traumatic, that the experience of the defeat led to pacifism. Indeed, the many Japanese peace movements which have developed since the last war are all based on the experience of Hiroshima and Nagasaki.

For this reason, the post-war desire to create an industrial structure based on advanced science and technology did not find expression in a strong military; rather it was focused entirely on rebuilding Japan as a modern industrial nation. As a result, a great deal of Japan's efforts have been put into economic growth based on export-oriented industries, which in turn are based on advanced science and technology. Some time in the 1970s, the Japanese more or less realised their goal, and they began to express their delight in being a 'developed,' 'rich,' 'high-technological,' and 'western' nation. And now, to be one of the seven Summit nations makes the Japanese not only self-complacent but arrogant as well. To be a member nation of a Summit as an economic power reminds them of their participation in the disarmament talks after World War I when they were then a military power.

But Japan's economic growth has been too rapid and in that sense too successful. Apart from anything else, this success has resulted in a huge trade surplus which has been sustained for many years; this in turn has resulted in Japanese industry and commerce investing its recently-acquired wealth overseas in all manner of things — from manufacturing plants to night clubs. As has been pointed out by so many people so many times, Japan has turned to economic colonialism after failing to achieve a colonialism based on military power.

Inevitably, both developed and developing nations are offended and have become increasingly angry. From the Japanese point of view, this is a most unpleasant outcome. Regardless of what they say and do, and regardless of whether or not what they say and do is right or wrong, they do realise that they are disliked and hated in various parts of the world. Yet the Japanese continue to show indecisive attitudes. Or to put it more accurately, they do not understand why other countries, especially the developed western nations, are angry.

The Japanese feelings could be summed up as follows: After the defeat, they gave up the desire of becoming a military superpower and became a peace-loving nation because the

Americans told them to do so. They concentrated their efforts on export-led industry and exported finished products, because the Americans advised them to do so. It was also the Americans who advised them to restrict their imports. So, they have been doing exactly what they were told to do by the Americans during the Occupation. Indeed, to borrow the words from the 12 April 1951 editorial of the *Asahi Shinbun* (quoted earlier) the Japanese have been 'walking the same road even more vigorously by simply following the direction' given by General MacArthur.

After becoming a 'developed' nation, the Japanese are producing and exporting high-technology products and investing overseas, because they think this is what an advanced western nation does. Yet they are accused and hated, and they cannot understand why. The reasoning in the Japanese mind may be put like this: 'We are doing exactly what any advanced western nation does. Why do you accuse us, therefore, of colonialism or imperialism? We are merely behaving like a successful capitalistic country.'

I think this response is very similar to the feeling the Japanese experienced when they were forced to return the Liaotung peninsula to China after the Sino-Japanese War under pressure from Russia, France, and Germany. You will recall that, at that time, the Japanese thought they were entitled to acquire the Liaotung peninsula because a western nation in a similar situation could acquire such a territory without question. Yet they were puzzled and became angry when they were prevented from doing so by the three western powers precisely because Japan behaved like a western nation, they thought. In the Japanese mind, there is a clear similarity between the Liaotung incident on the one hand and the issue of trade imbalance and economic expansionism on the other.

Defence Mechanisms

To be criticised and hated by other nations is not a pleasant experience. The Japanese response to this sort of attack involves several predictable defence mechanisms. For example, intellectualisation has been a regular fall-back response ever since criticisms were first made about the Japanese. At the present time, the Japanese are eagerly reading books about Japanese society, about the 'origins' of the Japanese people, the Japanese language, post-war economic growth, Japanese management, and so on. This is clearly one way of avoiding the need to think about the international issues and actually doing something about them. To read about the alleged 'uniqueness' of the Japanese, Japanese culture, the Japanese language, or even the anatomy of the Japanese brain, creates a mood of self-complacency, in which the Japanese are able to detach themselves from the reality of the global economy. Intellectualisation has been most consistently present in response to the issue of trade imbalance, probably because this is less dangerous than other forms of defence mechanisms.

However, through time, the Japanese began to rely on other defence mechanisms, which are more likely to offend other nations. Projection and displacement, for example, are seen. When the developed nations criticise Japanese employers for not allowing their employees to take annual paid holidays, Japanese employers and government officials alike respond as follows: 'We work hard and we love to work. We are a diligent and excellent people. We should be commended and admired for that. Yet you criticise us. We do not understand. It is not we but you who are to be blamed. You are lazy and your work-force is poorly educated and poorly motivated. You only think about holidays and play. You should blame yourself for the poor performance of your economy.'

In reality, Japanese workers do desire and wish to have paid holidays, but they also know quite well that they are forced to sacrifice their lives for their company, and they dare not ask for a holiday. A vice president of an engineering college told me: 'we do not allow our faculty members to take paid holidays more than three days in a row. Indeed, we discourage them to take holidays at all, because we believe that holidays are to be reserved for the days when the teacher or a member of his family might fall sick.' This vice president also gave an example in which a big, well-known company fired those employees who had taken most or tried most to take paid holidays when a recession came. But even the longest paid holidays were, I should add, in accordance with the law, which is only concerned with a week or ten days at most!

Interestingly enough, when less-developed nations such as South Korea, Taiwan, Singapore, or Hong Kong are seen more and more as threats to Japan in the area of, for example, the automobile industry or advanced electronics, the Japanese are quick to point out their 'cheap labour' due to the 'over-population' and 'poverty' of these nations. These accusations, of course, parallel exactly what the Japanese were forced to hear over and over again for several decades, and now they direct the same accusations against other Asian nations in the form of displacement. Such accusations come about because the Japanese place themselves in the category of the 'advanced western nations' and, as a result of identification, look at other Asian nations through the eyes of the West.

Such Japanese responses are already offensive enough to other nations; but on top of this the Japanese sometimes turn to reaction formation, which can be even more dangerous than projection or displacement as a source of international tension and conflict. As has been the case in the past, reaction formation here is derived from identification with the aggressor. That is, the envy and admiration for the West is reversed and turned into narcissistic chauvinism and racism. The positive evaluation of things Japanese in the form of healthy nationalism perhaps may be desirable for the Japanese, who during much of their history suffered from the feeling of inferiority under the influence of the continental cultures and of the West. They probably need a more objective and positive image of themselves.

But when this is expressed in the form of narcissistic chauvinism and racism derived from reaction formation, there is reason to be cautious and apprehensive. Since reaction formation is a reversal of the attitudes previously held, the intensity of the reversed attitude is likely to be proportional to the intensity of the previous attitude. We may say that the stronger the extent of identification with the aggressor, the stronger the extent of chauvinism and racism, and this is a justifiable reason to be apprehensive.

I hope you will recall Takayama Chogyu and his *Nihon Shugi* ('Japanism'). I hope you will also recall the radical change of attitudes in the writings of Tokutomi Soho — to give only two examples. In both cases, the excessive worship of the West was reversed into an opposite extreme which manifested itself in chauvinism and racism. As I mentioned in Chapters 5 and 6, the inherent ideology of this response was gradually taken on board by the Japanese government and the military and became the official doctrine supporting Japan's cause in the Pacific war.

We might also argue that the western rejection of Japan after the Sino-Japanese War, the Russo-Japanese War, and World War I is comparable to the western criticisms and anger against Japan over the trade issues of the 1980s. From the Japanese point of view, both are forms of unjustifiable intimidation which in their opinion must be rigorously counter-attacked. Indeed, chauvinistic and racist opinions have already begun to be expressed against the West and other Asian countries in connection with trade imbalances and economic expansionism; indeed, former Prime Minister Nakasone Yasuhiro became internationally famous for a statement he made when in office, which was generally interpreted as racist by non-Japanese.

To many Asians, Japan's economic expansionism is seen as another form of Japanese colonialism; colonialism based on economic power rather than military power. The disguised colonialism vividly reminds them of the nightmare they endured during World War II. In the early 1980s, when the Japanese Ministry of Education forced textbook publishers to delete or modify the descriptions of what the Imperial Japanese Forces did in Asia during the war, many Asian countries, especially China and Korea, reacted violently. Yet the Ministry of Education maintains a policy of covering up the massacres and atrocities as much as possible. Psychoanalytically, this is a denial; the Ministry of Education is trying to say that such incidents did not happen. This attitude reminds us of the post-war neo-Nazis in West Germany, who insist that concentration camps did not exist and this is a fabrication made up by Jews. Some of the accusations made by other countries against Japan (for example, dumping) are also dealt with by the Japanese by means of denial.

Future of the Japanese

At this point, let us speculate about the future of the Japanese. Assuming that Japan will continue to be confronted from time to time by external threats and unpleasant experiences, the Japanese are likely to respond to these events psychoanalytically as before. Among the various defence mechanisms, the extent of resorting to identification with the aggressor in the future will depend on the power of the Japanese economy at the time and also on the possibility of turning economic power into military power. It is conceivable that, as one of the possibilities, by considering the strengh of their economy, the Japanese may identify with the West less and less in the future.

Certainly, it has become much more difficult to scare or frighten the Japanese. This is not only because a strong economy *per se* is power, but also because it could be turned into a military superpower at any time quite easily, as many Asians fear consistently. In order to scare the Japanese, extensive military threats would be needed, but because of the exterminating effect of nuclear weapons, the military superpowers have become much more cautious about getting involved in a war, despite their continued preparation for a war. As we move towards the end of the twentieth century it is seen as increasingly difficult by the industrialised world as a whole to justify a large-scale war simply because of disputes over trade issues. This all means that to scare the Japanese militarily or to make another nuclear attack on Japan is virtually inconceivable in the context of a world view of decency and common sense.

To threaten the Japanese economy is not easy either. Two conceivable measures are a trade embargo and higher tariffs on Japanese products. But history repeatedly tells us that a trade embargo is not as effective as we like to assume. To implement an embargo on oil and foodstuffs, for example, may not be so threatening to the Japanese. Higher tariffs are conceivably much more effective, but in the world after the Great Depression of the 1930s, both politicians and economists know only too well that the principle of free trade must be maintained at all costs. For this reason, no advanced country could consider introducing and maintaining an effective protectionist policy, although the pressures to do so will always exist in the West. No western political leader has ever rejected the GATT. The Japanese themselves know all about this; which is one of the reasons why they are not afraid of protectionism even though government sources may protest about such considerations amongst western countries.

Thus, to threaten the Japanese effectively is not as easy as it was in the mid-nineteenth century or indeed in the early part of the twentieth century. Rather, the focus of interest for us now is how long the Japanese continue to dwell upon identification with the aggressor after the aggressor is no longer seen as aggressor.

If and when this defence mechanism ceases to be the most important one in the minds of the Japanese, we may expect that, in future when they are criticised, they will counter-attack in less chauvinistic and racialist terms, because this form of response is a reaction formation by reversing identification with the aggressor. Of course, this statement must be conditional. If the Japanese think they are attacked in racialist terms as was the case in the 1920s and 1930s, they are most likely to respond in racialist terms.

Without identification with the aggressor, Japan's role in international politics may possibly become similar to that of the United States, which is characterised by projection, displacement and denial, accompanied by power display. There are two reasons to support such a speculation. First, as an advanced capitalistic economy, Japan has indeed become similar to the United States, partly as a result of identification, but also partly due to the fact of economic growth *per se*.

Second, both the United States and Japan have suffered from feelings of inferiority for a long time which somehow must be made up. Most Americans at least in the past suffered from the fact that they were poor, unsuccessful Europeans or descendents of such Europeans. If we take the view of the psychoanalyst Alfred Adler, the American love of power and power display can easily be seen as an effort to make up for this miserable handicap. In the case of the Japanese, of course, their backwardness and weakness which other countries took advantage of are what they must make up. In response to the western threat, the Japanese tried to fight back by means of a modern military. After this failure they tried to make up for their inferior position by economic growth. This strategy has succeeded, and the Japanese can now boast about their economic power. Thus, like the Americans, the Japanese are today in a position to resort to power display, if they so wish. Because of these two important similarities between the United States and Japan, in the future the Japanese, like the Americans, may well decide to defend themselves by means of power and power display. I believe this option is a distinct possibility.

More Questions

Although I have used a psychoanalytical approach in this book, I am not saying that this is the only way to understand Japanese culture. Nor do I say this approach can explain most of Japanese culture. I do not wish to be that dogmatic. All I am saying is that, by looking at Japanese culture from a psychoanalytical point of view, a variety of diverse phenomena in Japanese culture in the past and at present can be interpreted with some consistency. In this sense, such an approach does have a certain value.

If we look at a variety of other cultures, we begin to realise that the Japanese are probably not the only people in the world who have applied psychoanalytical defence mechanisms in dealing with the threat of more powerful cultures. Look at the Philippines, for example, where the natives say: 'Yankee go home; and take me with you!' I can also recognise phenomena similar to the ones I have discussed in this book in Hong Kong, and to a lesser extent in Korea and Taiwan. Many western European countries, especially West Germany, the Netherlands, and the Scandinavian countries show considerable identification with the Americans. Even communist countries such as Hungary and Poland could be added to the list. A logical explanation is the power of the Americans.

It is interesting to reflect on the fact that the Americans have not changed at all in over 100 years. The Americans love power and power display. In all forms of international negotiations, they try to influence others by displaying power. Commodore Perry did. Consul General Harris did. General MacArthur did. After World War II, the Americans displayed power in dealing with the Soviet Union, Cuba, Libya, or Nicaragua. No wonder identification with the Americans is seen in so many countries.

But at the same time, we must realise that the human mind is not that simple. Not everyone who has been exposed to a powerful people identifies with them. For example, in Ethiopia, which was occupied by Italy during World War II, both pro-Italians and anti-Italians are to be found amongst those who have had closest contact with the Italians. Similarly, among the Koreans who have had most contact with the Japanese and suffered from their oppression, there are both pro-Japanese and anti-Japanese Koreans. Evidently, we must take the factor of personality differences into account. Two people in an identical situation may not resort to the same defence mechanisms.

There are many nationalities and peoples who have suffered from invasion, occupation, or colonialism. But extensive identification with the aggressor is not necessarily seen. Often western-educated leaders, such as Gandhi or Nehru, become nationalistic. The former colonial countries are no more westernised than Japan.

These facts lead us to a series of new questions. Are the Japanese more prone to identify with the aggressor? If so, why? Is this due to the way Japanese children are raised? Or because the Japanese never valued their own culture highly? Does identification with the aggressor take place under some specific conditions? For example, power display without oppression? Was this condition maximally found in the case of Japan? I am not qualified to answer these questions, but I hope this book has aroused your interest in studying culture psychoanalytically.

APPENDIX
How We Respond to Threat: Nine Defence Mechanisms

PSYCHOANALYSIS was originated by a remarkable Jewish Austrian medical doctor by the name of Sigmund Freud (1856-1939). He was remarkable because he drew our attention to the effects of conflict and stress within our minds. His approach to our thought processes was bold and innovative, and for this reason, Freud is often compared with such influential modern thinkers as Darwin, Marx, and Einstein. Predictably, Freud has attracted considerable criticism. For example, he has been criticised repeatedly for placing too much emphasis on sex.

Much of psychoanalytic literature is very technical and complex. Almost every psychoanalytical book is full of jargon which the layman cannot understand. But this does not mean that what psychoanalysis is saying is irrelevant to our daily lives. On the contrary, psychoanalysis deals with the essence of our existence, and if we translate psychoanalysis into a plain and simple language, almost anyone can understand the psychoanalytical perspective and its importance in understanding ourselves. And that is what I am going to do first of all here: I am going to restate and explain some aspects of psychoanalysis in an understandable language, from which we can then go on to explore Japanese culture psychoanalytically.

Defence Mechanisms? What Are They?

The part of psychoanalysis in which I am interested in this book is called 'defence mechanisms.' Defence mechanisms consist of a variety of responses which we employ in our minds from time to time.

The reason why we use defence mechanisms may be stated like this: Since we do not live in a utopia or paradise (at least most of us!), we are always faced with the harsh reality of everyday living. We work hard to live, and we encounter many unpleasant experiences. We often fail, make mistakes, and miss out on opportunities. Not only that, others take advantage of us. They ridicule and laugh at our weaknesses.

What can a person do in such a situation? Well, most of us value ourselves, and when we are attacked, we try to defend ourselves. We defend ourselves psychologically by manipulating our thought processes. In this way, we try to reduce or eliminate the shock of unpleasant events. We try to maintain the integrity of ourselves psychologically by means of these thought processes. These processes are what are known as defence mechanisms.

There are many defence mechanisms known in psychoanalysis, but I would like to mention and explain only nine of them here.

Denial This is a defence mechanism we often use. A person denies the reality of the objective world. He or she refuses to admit that a disturbing fact does exist. For example, upon hearing the news of the assassination of President Kennedy, many Americans said: 'No! That can't be true!' Another example is a mother who refuses to accept that her child is no longer alive after a fatal accident.

Denial is a childish and ineffective defence mechanism because you deny reality. No matter how you try to convince yourself, the fact remains. By means of denial, perhaps you can reduce the impact of the shock, but sooner or later you have to accept the fact.

Projection By this method, a person believes that others are to be blamed. For example, when a man hates another man, he says: 'He hates me,' instead of 'I hate him,' because to hate other people is not a nice thing. To have an undesirable trait such as hating people is disturbing, and in order to defend the dignity of the self, the undesirable trait is 'projected' onto another person who, in turn, becomes the bad guy.

This is a dangerous defence mechanism because you are likely to offend others. You refuse to admit that you are wrong. Not only that, you criticise others for negative character traits which actually are your own.

Displacement Projection is often seen with another defence mechanism called 'displacement.' When a person cannot release his energy for action in a satisfactory way, he finds another channel to release it. There are many ways to do that, but if we limit our focus on the situations where a person projects an objectionable thought or action onto another person, he may actually attack that person. Usually a weak and innocent individual is chosen as a victim, because to attack someone who is powerful is dangerous. Here, displacement comes after projection.

It is easy to find many examples of displacement in our daily lives. Indeed, when we become irritated and frustrated, we quite often use displacement. For example, when a man is frustrated at his job because of a bad relationship with his boss, he usually cannot fight back, and instead of attacking the boss, he beats his wife at home. Or when a man loses his job, he may be able to do nothing to change the situation. In order to release his anger and frustration, he may pick on a member of a minority group who has nothing to do with his job and make a malicious remark. He may even attack him physically. Unfortunately, incidents like these happen over and over again in our daily lives. The object for displacement need not be a person. It can be a dog, instead of wife, or a material object instead of a member of a minority.

Isolation In this case, feelings and emotions are eliminated from a person's thoughts. One sees, acts, and responds like a robot. A human being usually is full of feelings and emotions. We become happy, glad, or delighted when something nice happens, and we become sad or depressed when a bad thing happens. We also become angry, furious, fearful, or desperate. These are our characteristics as an advanced primate species.

To have a variety of feelings and emotions enriches our lives, and precisely for this reason, we have produced novels, poems, paintings, operas, chamber music, and many other art forms. Any music-lover understands the intensity of feeling and emotion which Bach's keyboard music or Bruckner's symphony arouses in our minds.

When our feelings and emotions are pleasant or delightful, we enjoy, and we want more. But, on the other hand, when we experience emotions of fear or desperation, we seek to avoid them. One way of doing so is to eliminate feelings and emotions from our thoughts. In this way, a fearful or desperate notion becomes merely an idea; nothing else. The close connection between the idea and a feeling of fear is disconnected by means of a psychological manipulation. The idea now exists in isolation without emotion. You can think about it without shedding tears.

Perhaps this defence mechanism is hard to understand, but people placed in an extreme situation often show isolation. For example, a person who has lost his home, fortune, and family by a fire often becomes totally emotionless. Indeed, the faces of people in a disaster area after an earthquake, tornado, hurricane, or flood are quite often totally devoid of emotion.

Rationalisation Perhaps this is the best known defence mechanism, and in fact many of us seriously or jokingly explain our behaviour by means of 'rationalisation.' Here, a person finds a plausible justification in order to explain away a certain disturbing phenomenon. Superficially, such an explanation sounds reasonable, but if a third person looks at the situation, the explanation is incorrect. For example, a smoker does not quit smoking despite the fact that he knows smoking is dangerous to his (and others') health, but responds by saying that if he quits smoking, he would eat more instead, and being overweight is more dangerous and bad for the heart. In this way, a person can justify his behaviour which otherwise is disturbing. It is always easy to 'rationalise,' because we can always find a plausible reason in order to explain our behaviour. Similarly, a person can commit an immoral or unethical act and justify that.

Intellectualisation Intellectualisation is similar to rationalisation, but in intellectualisation, feelings and emotions are eliminated, or 'isolated.' A person explains a danger coldly without any sense of fear, as if he were talking about somebody else's problem. Often he uses many scholarly or scientific words to describe the situation. Sometimes, his scientific explanation can be quite correct and accurate. By assuming an objective, third-person position without emotion in order to look at one's own problem, one reduces the intensity of the danger in reality.

For example, a medical doctor dying of cancer can talk about the condition of his illness in detail every day, explaining how the condition is getting worse and worse as time goes by. He may also predict the date when he dies. He assumes the position of a professor explaining the condition of his patient to his students.

Regression When a person becomes frustrated, he may indulge in rather childish behaviour. This is another defence mechanism called 'regression.' Psychoanalysts assume that a person has a tendency to revert to an earlier stage of development when (he thinks) he had a better life. By trying to revert to the 'good old days' when there were no problems, a person attempts to avoid the difficulty he is faced with in the present.

For example, a 23-year-old, college-educated professional woman may start collecting a large number of dolls for children as a result of a complicated relationship with a man which she cannot solve. She may devote all her available time and energy to collecting and playing with the dolls, as if she were a child. Of course, regression is not limited to women. A mature, middle-aged man may also regress. After a frustrating day at his office, a businessman may talk and behave like a child towards his wife.

A child may regress to an even earlier stage. A phenomenon which many parents observe at home occurs when the second child is born. At this point, the first child quite often regresses. Why? Because when he was the only child, his parents gave him their undivided attention. It was paradise. But when the younger sibling is born, the older child's 'paradise' is compromised as a result of much parental attention now being directed to the new arrival. This results in a crisis. In such a situation, a six-year-old boy, for example, may begin refusing to wear shoes.

Reaction Formation When a person experiences tension because of the nature of his particular thought or action, one way to reduce such tension is to totally change his thought or action. He can do this most effectively by completely reversing his previous thought or action. This does not mean that he has changed his personality. On the contrary, he is likely to remain very much the same person. Unconsciously, he probably has the same thoughts as before, but superficially, he now appears (to himself) to be different.

For example, suppose a mother hates her child. But the fact that she hates her own child is unacceptable to her. She considers herself a well-educated, respectable woman. Here, what she can do is to reverse her hatred and love her child instead. To recognise that she loves her child is acceptable and wonderful. As in this case, reaction formation is a defence mechanism in which a person defends his integrity by reversing his thought or action.

Similarly, a prejudiced person may become overtly friendly towards members of a minority group he hates, or a suitor may suddenly begin to tell everyone that he hates the woman whom he courted unsuccessfully. In both cases, a person defends himself by means of reaction formation. Here, 'hate' becomes 'love,' and 'love' becomes 'hate,' and tension is reduced.

Since reaction formation involves the reversal of the previous thought, it may require a conscious effort to convince oneself. Such an effort may look quite unnatural and overdone in terms of common sense. For example, a mother may become over-affectionate and buy expensive toys which she cannot afford. Or a busy man devotes his available time to an anti-discrimination movement, disregarding his family. In the case of the unsuccessful suitor, he may explain in detail how ugly and stupid the woman actually is.

Reaction formation can be seen in many distressing situations. A widow may be cheerful and smiling after the funeral of her husband, or a man may become unusually talkative and laugh a lot the day before he commits suicide. Some cultures encourage reaction formation through smiling, laughter, and humour upon encountering painful or distressing situations. I think a good example in this respect is Japanese culture.

Identification with the aggressor The substance of this book revolves around this last but most important defence mechanism. I would even go as far as to say that through a good understanding of this particular behavioural response you will gain an entirely new perspective and considerable insight into the Japanese culture and its people.

This defence mechanism was presented and discussed by Freud as the core of his psychoanalytic thinking. According to Freud, a little boy loves his mother, but he realises that his father also loves her. He is a rival. Besides, the father is much bigger and stronger. There is no chance for the little boy to defeat his father and win the mother. Yet he loves her. What can he do? This is the well-known theory of the Oedipus conflict.

Freud thinks that the solution for the boy out of this miserable situation is to identify with his father. 'Identification' here refers to both the process and result of placing oneself in another's position through imagination and understanding. *One imagines oneself to be somebody else and tries to think and feel like him.*

Well, what happens when a little boy who finds himself in such a miserable situation does this? When he identifies with his father, he places himself in his father's position, and from this perspective, he can love his mother. At the same time, he is no longer weak and miserable, because he now thinks and feels like his father. After identification, he is big and strong, and he can love the woman in his life. This is a wonderful solution. Furthermore, there is an additional bonus to it. He is praised for obeying his father's orders. Since the boy thinks and feels like his father, what his father wants him to do is actually what he himself wants to do; what his father does not want him to do is what he does not want to do either. In effect, the boy obeys his father's orders, and he is loved by his father for being a good boy.

Identification with the aggressor as a defence mechanism was further developed by Anna Freud, Sigmund Freud's daughter. According to her, identification with the aggressor can be observed in a variety of situations. She talks about a case of an elementary school boy who had a habit of making faces when he was scolded by his teacher. The teacher thought that either the boy was consciously making fun of him or else he had an involuntary tic on his face. A psychoanalytical examination revealed that the boy identified himself with the teacher when he was scolded and imitated his expression involuntarily.

Another clinical example given by Anna Freud deals with a girl who was afraid of ghosts. Suddenly, however, she got a splendid idea for overcoming her fear. When she had to cross the hall at home in the dark, she made all kinds of strange gestures as she went. She explained: 'There is no need to be afraid in the hall. You just have to pretend that you are the ghost who might meet you.' Here, by making strange gestures, she herself became a ghost. Since she is a ghost, she need not be afraid of another ghost. By impersonating the aggressor, a threatened person can transform himself into the person (or the ghost) who makes the threat. If you carry on this process, you yourself become aggressive and begin attacking others. For example, a member of a minority group may become very harsh and critical towards his own group.

Prisoners in Concentration Camps

Probably the most extreme form of identification with the aggressor is to be found in a study by Bruno Bettelheim. Bettelheim himself is Jewish and survived two concentration camps during 1938-39. After this experience, he published what he had seen inside the concentration camps. Being a psychoanalyst himself, Bettelheim's psychoanalytic description of the prisoners is sharp and illuminating. The study provides a vivid account of how a person thinks and responds when placed in an extreme situation.

Put very simply, the Gestapo's main goal was to produce in the prisoners childlike attitudes and childlike dependency, so that they could be handled and manipulated at will. After the initial shock of being in a concentration camp and various attempts to deal with the situation, the prisoners began to exhibit infantile behaviour patterns; that is, they regressed.

In the beginning, childlike behaviour was forced upon them. They were forced to say 'thou' (*du*) to one another, and in Germany, only small children and intimates used this expression. Titles are very important in German culture, but the prisoners were not allowed to use titles to each other. Instead, they were forced to address the guards in the most deferential manner, giving them all their titles.

The prisoners were also forced to perform childish acts. For example, they were told to carry heavy stones from one place to another and back to the place where they had picked them up. They were told to dig holes in the ground with their bare hands, although tools were available. They were required to obtain the guard's permission before going to the toilet. The Gestapo punished the whole group when one member misbehaved. As a result, those who did not develop a childlike dependency on the guards were criticised by fellow prisoners. Bettelheim thinks that there developed between them a relationship of a cruel and domineering father (the guard) and a helpless child (the prisoner).

In the final stage of adjustment to the camp, prisoners began to think and behave like the Gestapo. Old prisoners, who had been in the camp for several years, behaved like the Gestapo and sometimes their behaviour was worse than that of the Gestapo. For example, old prisoners tortured disobedient prisoners for days and slowly killed them by copying the Gestapo methods. One of the guards' leisure-time activities was to find out who could stand to be hit longest without uttering a complaint. Old prisoners copied this behaviour, and played the same 'game' on their fellow prisoners.

The Gestapo were always enforcing new rules, which often originated as the whims of a guard. These rules were usually forgotten as soon as they were formulated. But there were always some old prisoners who continued to follow them and tried to enforce them on the others long after the Gestapo had forgotten about them.

Some old prisoners even tried to acquire old pieces of Gestapo uniforms. If unsuccessful, they tried to sew and mend their uniforms so that they would resemble the uniforms of the guards. When asked why they did it, they answered that they wanted to look like the guards.

Bettelheim thinks that regressed prisoners developed their own image of the Gestapo members as their 'fathers.' They reasoned that all-powerful 'fathers' should be just and kind. They insisted that behind their rough exteriors, the Gestapo officers had a feeling of justice and propriety and they were even trying to help the prisoners. In reality, no one ever experienced helpful behaviour from a Gestapo officer, and this was explained by saying that they were successfully hiding their true feelings because otherwise they would not be able to help the prisoners.

From all of this about concentration camps many other inferences can be drawn. We can understand how people respond and try to deal with an extreme situation in which they are totally powerless and helpless. It is sad to have to admit that old prisoners thought and behaved like the Gestapo officers because for them, that might have been the only way to survive. At least, identification with the aggressor was likely to be the most effective defence mechanism for them.

The Japanese and Defence Mechanisms

So far, I have presented and discussed nine defence mechanisms and these are the only psychoanalytical concepts used in this book. I shall now consider Japanese culture, both past and present, by applying these concepts. As I said earlier, identification with the aggressor is the most important defence mechanism that concerns us here. Of course, the Japanese have never found themselves in a situation as extreme as that of the Jews in the concentration camps. But it is important to realise that whenever a people are threatened by another people more powerful than themselves, identification with the aggressor as a possible defence mechanism exists. My contention is that the Japanese have been experiencing the threat of more powerful peoples throughout much of their history and as a result, the Japanese have systematically dealt with their anxiety by identifying with the aggressor.

In the beginning of Japanese history, the peoples of the continent and the Korean peninsula were technologically more advanced, and the power and prestige of these peoples, especially the Chinese, were intensely felt by the Japanese. The Japanese identified with them, and accepted and imitated their cultures eagerly. In the sixteenth century, Europeans began to appear as peoples of advanced technology, and later they were joined by Americans as another advanced people with power and technology. In the middle of the nineteenth century, by displaying power and threat consistently in a well calculated manner, Commodore Perry succeeded in opening Japan to the rest of the world.

The Japanese identified with the westerners and became westernised actively and intentionally. After acquiring a modern military around the turn of the century, the Japanese began to look at themselves as a 'western' colonising power. But they realised that they were rejected by the West precisely because of their identification with the West. They tried various defence mechanisms to deal with the problem. Through time, the belief in Japanese superiority in the form of reaction formation became the dominant political ideology, and this was the ideology of Japanese militarism and expansionism until the end of World War II.

The defeat in World War II was an intense shock to the Japanese, and they employed a variety of defence mechanisms to minimise the reality of defeat. General Douglas MacArthur administered occupied Japan as an authoritarian yet paternalistic Supreme Commander-in-Chief, and the Japanese were forced to realise that MacArthur existed over and above the Emperor.

Until the end of the war, the Japanese conceived of their relationship with the Emperor in terms of the extension of the parent-child relationship. Since MacArthur war paternalistic and above the Emperor, the Japanese began to look at him as a new father figure. For his part, MacArthur conceived of himself as the guardian of the Japanese who in his opinion were infantile. The Japanese began to identify with him and later with the Americans as a whole. They became very much 'Americanised.' A huge trade surplus has offended both the developed and developing nations in recent years, and the Japanese have tried to deal with the problem by means of, for example, intellectualisation.

Notes

Chapter 1 CHINA AND KOREA AND JAPAN

[1]All quotations from sources written in the Japanese and Chinese languages were translated into English by me. The Emperor's rescript in accepting the Joint Declaration in 1945 was quoted from the official English version, and letters to General MacArthur written in English were quoted in the original form.

Chapter 3 TWO TREATIES AND THE MEIJI RESTORATION

[1]Preble thought that the Japanese were lewd. He wrote as follows in his diary (George Henry Preble, *The Opening of Japan: A Diary of Discovery in the Far East, 1853-1856*, B. Szczesniak, ed., Norman: University of Oklahoma Press, 1962): 'Among the presents received by Com. Perry, was a box of obscene paintings of naked men and women, another proof of the lewdness of this exclusive people [p. 126).' 'Another instance of this people's sensuality occurred at the meeting today. Capt A[bbott] remarking to the interpreter that it was a rainy day. Yes, said he, a fine day for lieing [sic] with the ladies [p. 137].'

Chapter 8 GENERAL MACARTHUR: THE NEW EMPEROR FROM AMERICA

[1]MacArthur writes what he saw when he offered the Emperor a cigarette: 'I noticed how his hands shook as I lighted it for him. I tried to make it as easy for him as I could, but I knew how deep and dreadful must be his agony of humiliation.' See Douglas MacArthur, *Reminiscences*, New York: McGraw-Hill, 1964, pp. 287-288.

[2]In connection with the Lockheed scandal, when it was revealed that Kodama Yoshio, a very influential, die-hard right-wing activist, was actually a CIA agent, most Japanese were flabbergasted. But in view of this cultural background of the 'parent-child' relationship, it would have been very easy for him to establish such a relationship with Americans.

Chapter 10 POPULAR CULTURE IN JAPAN

[1]A similar phenomenon is seen at a Catholic university in Tokyo, in which some courses are taught in English. There is an unspoken policy to employ Caucasians preferentially as its faculty members without selecting them on the basis of scholarly excellence. In this sense, this university is very 'Japanese,' because Japanese universities are often dumping grounds for old, incompetent, or useless bureaucrats or journalists without scholarly publications and without a Ph.D. A grade school teacher can get a university position, too, if he or she knows the 'right' person.

References

In order to save space, only the most relevant works are listed here. For a more detailed bibliography, see my journal articles referred to below.

INTRODUCTION

For the psychiatric study of Mishima's suicide mentioned in the text, see, Robert Jay Lifton, *The Broken Connection*, New York: Simon and Schuster, 1979.

Chapter 1 CHINA AND KOREA AND JAPAN

For Chinese observations about Japanese culture, see Sanetou Keishu, 'Chugokujin no nihonkan,' pp. 327-345 in *Nihon Bunka to Chugoku*, Bito Masahide, ed., Tokyo: Taishu Kan, 1968.

The information on the total number of missions to China varies considerably from one source to another. I quoted from 'Kaisetsu,' p. 15 in Wada Kiyoshi and Ishihara Michihiro, eds., *Kutojyo Wakoku Nihon Den, Soshi Nihon Den, Genshi Nihon Den*, Tokyo: Iwanami Shoten, 1956. But other sources give us different information. For example, *Kodansha Encyclopedia of Japan* Vol. 7, Tokyo: Kodansha, 1983, pp. 259-260, suggests that between 600 and 840, at least 19 missions were sent to China. The informatiion on the total number of students and classification of the people on board was taken from Wakamori Taro and Takahashi Shinichi, eds., *Nihon Rekishi o Saguru*, Tokyo: Kawade Shobo Shinsha, 1963, p. 47.

The scholarly debate took place between Ujisafu Yorinaga and Fujiwara Michinori on June 7, Tenyo 2 (1145). See, Fujiwara Yorinaga, *Daiki*, Vol. 1, Kyoto: Rinkawa Shoten, 1966, p. 154.

For the practice of travelling to Nagasaki among scholars in Edo, see Hirakawa Sukehiro, *Wakon Yosai no Keifu*, Tokyo: Kawade Shobo Shinsha, 1976, p. 40.

For other sources, see Michio Kitahara, 'Japanese attitudes toward the Chinese and the Koreans in history,' *Sociologia Internationalis*, Vol. 25, No. 1, 1987, pp. 85-96.

Chapter 2 COMMODORE PERRY: A DRAMA OF POWER DISPLAY

Perry's letter to Secretary of the Navy is reprinted in *Message of the President of the United States*, Senate, 33rd Congress, 2nd Session, Ex. Doc. No. 34, pp. 12-14. Perry's diary is edited by R. Pineau and published as *The Japan Expedition 1852-1854*, Washington D.C.: Smithsonian Institution Press, 1968.

For the dramaturgical approach in sociology, see Erving Goffman, *The Presentation of Self in Everyday Life*, Garden City: Double Day Anchor Books, 1959.

For other sources, see Michio Kitahara 'Commodore Perry and the Japanese: A Study in the Dramaturgy of Power,' *Symbolic Interaction*, Vol. 9, No. 1, 1986, pp. 53-65.

Chapter 3 TWO TREATIES AND THE MEIJI RESTORATION

For suggestions and proposals in response to Perry's demand, see Shimazu Nariakira, 'Jyosho,' pp. 636-638 in Vol. 1, Ii Naosuke, 'Beikoku kokusho ni tsuite,' p. 255-259; and Mori Yoshichika, 'Jyosho,' pp. 260-261 in Vol. 2, and Okudaira Masamoto, 'Jyosho,' pp. 593-594 in Vol. 3 of *Bakumatsu Gaikokukankei Bunsho*, Shiryo Hensanjyo, ed., Tokyo: Tokyo Daigaku Shuppan Kai, 1972; Mito Nariaki, 'Kaibo Guson,' pp. 9-18, and Kuroda Nagahiro, 'Jyosho,' pp. 27-35 in *Bakumatsu Seijiron Shu*, Yoshida Tsunekichi and Sato Seizaburo, eds., Tokyo: Iwanami Shoten, 1976; and Sanjyo Sanetsumu, *Sanjyo Sanetsumu Shuroku*, Vol. 2, Nihon Shiseki Kyokai, ed., Tokyo: Tokyo Daigaku Shuppan Kai, 1972, pp. 84-89. See also Watanuki Tetsuo, *Ishin to Kakumei*, Vol. 1, Tokyo: Taimeido, 1973, p. 229.

The published diaries by Perry's crew members are S. Wells Williams, *A Journal of the Perry Expedition to Japan*, F. W. Williams, ed., Wilmington, Delaware and London: Scholarly Resources, Inc., 1973; Francis L. Hawks, *Narrative of the Expedition of an American Squadron to the China Seas and Japan, Performed in the years 1852-1854*. New York: D. Appleton & Co., 1857; and George Henry Preble, *The Opening of Japan: A Diary of Discovery in the Far East, 1853-1856*, Boleslaw Szczesniak, ed., Norman: University of Oklahoma Press, 1962, see pp. 119-120, and p. 123.

For anti-western responses, see Ohashi Totsuan, 'Seiken kaifuku hisaku,' in *Bakumatsu Seijiron Shu*, Yoshida Tsunekichi and Sato Scizaburo, eds., Tokyo: Iwanami Shoten, 1976, pp. 188-205; Kusaka Genzui, 'Kaiwan chigen,' in *Nihon Shiso no Keifu, Ge*, Odamura Torajiro, ed., Tokyo: Jiji Tsushin Sha, 1971, pp. 161-166; Francis Ottiwell Adams, *The History of Japan*, Vol. 1, London: Henry S. King, 1874, pp. 124, 128, 133, 155, 191-193, 232, 262, 373, 485; Ernest Satow, *A Diplomat in Japan*, Tokyo: Oxford University Press, 1968, p. 46, 88-89, 105-115; Godai Saisuke, 'Jyoshin sho,' in *Sappan Kaigun Shi, Chukan*, Shimazuke Hensanjyo, ed., Tokyo: Hara Shobo, 1968, pp. 867-886.

For other sources, see Michio Kitahara, 'Commodore Perry and the Japanese: A Study in the Dramaturgy of Power,' *Symbolic Interaction*, Vol. 9, No. 1, 1986, pp. 53-65.

Chapter 4 PROCESSES OF WESTERNISATION

For the history of *wakon yosai*, see *Tetsugaku Jiten*, Shimonaka Kunihiko, ed., Tokyo: Heibon Sha, 1971, pp. 1535-1536. Other sources are found in Michio Kitahara, 'The rise of four mottoes in Japan before and after the Meiji Restoration,' *Journal of Asian History*, Vol. 20, No. 1, 1986, pp. 54-64.

Chapter 5 UNSUCCESSFUL IDENTIFICATION

Regarding the issue of westerners living among Japanese, see Ueki Edamori, *Jyoyaku Kaisei Ikani*, Tokyo: Author, 1889; Kato Hiroyuki, *Zakkyo Sosyo*, Tokyo: Tetsugaku Shoin, 1893; Inouye Tetsujiro, 'Naichi Zakkyo Ron,' pp. 471-488 in *Naichi Zakkyo Ron*, 2 Vols., Ohashi Yasujiro, ed., Tokyo: Tetsugaku Shoin, 1889 and 1891; Suzuki Junichiro, *Naichi Zakkyo Kokoroe*, Tokyo: Fukuroya Shoten, 1894.

Takahashi Yoshio's argument for intermarriage is found in his *Nihonjinshu Kairyo Ron*, Tokyo: Ishikawa Hanjiro, 1884. Mori Arinori's view is mentioned in Nagai Michio, 'Mori Arinori,' pp. 111-122 in *Shinpan Nihon no Shisoka, Jyo*, Asahi Jyanaru, ed., Tokyo: Asahi Shinbun Sha, 1975. See p. 115.

Kato Hiroyuki's sarcastic view is found in his 'Nihonjin no Seihitsu,' *Nihonjin*, Vol. 4, 1888, pp. 172-177.

Aizawa Yasushi's argument for an alliance with China, see his *Shinron*, Edo: Edo Shorin Gyokusan Do, 1825.

For early colonialistic views, see Takegoshi Yosaburo, *Shina Ron*, Tokyo: Minyu Sha, 1894, p. 87; and Okuma Shigenobu, *Okuma Haku Shakai Kan*, Tokyo: Bunsei Sha, 1910, pp. 87-88.

The massacre of Korean residents in Japan is described in details in Duck Sang Gang and Seoung Dong Gum, *Kanto Dai Shinsai to Chosenjin*. Tokyo: Misuzu Shobo, 1963. The information on the number of Koreans 'protected' and the length of 'protection' was obtained from Iyenaga Saburo, ed., *Nihon Shi Shiryo, Jyokan*, Tokyo: Tokyo Horei Shuppan, 1973, p. 620.

For other sources, see Michio Kitahara, 'Psychoanalytic aspects of Japanese militarism," *International Interactions*, Vol. 12, No. 1, 1985, pp. 1-20.

Chapter 6 WESTERN REJECTION AND WORLD WAR II

The information on right-wing extremist organisations can be found in Watanabe Kijiro, *Taiheiyo Senso no Rekishiteki Kosatsu*, Tokyo: Toyo Keizai Shinpo Sha, 1947, p. 115-123; Hashikawa Bunzo, *Kindai Nihon Seiji Shiso no Shoso*, Tokyo: Mirai Sha, 1968, pp. 238-242.

For the official doctrine of Japan as a 'Divine Land' as expressed by the Ministry of Education, see Monbu Sho Kyogaku Kyoku, 'Kokutai no Hongi,' pp. 69-90, and 'Shinmin no Michi,' pp. 157-187, in *Showa Shiso Shu*, II, Hashikawa Bunzo, ed., Tokyo: Chikuma Shobo, 1978. For other sources, see Michio Kitahara, 'Psychoanalytic aspects of Japanese militarism,' *International Interactions*, Vol. 12, No. 1, 1985, pp. 1-20.

Chapter 7 SHOCK OF THE DEFEAT

Ensign John M. O'Connell's diary of September, 1945 was quoted from John Curtis Perry, *Beneath the Eagle's Wings*, New York: Dodd, Mead and Co., 1980, p. 106.

For Japanese resistance and defiance to the occupation, see Anonymous, 'Japanese asks us for "fair" regime,' *New York Times*, 1 September 1945, p. 2; F. L. Kluckhohn, 'Japan's premier explains defeat,' *New York Times*, 6 September 1945, pp. 1 and 3.

For Japanese 'cold treatment,' see Frank L. Kluckhohn, 'Japanese bitter in defeat; angered by raids on Tokyo,' *New York Times*, 1 September 1945.

For other sources, see Michio Kitahara, 'Japanese responses to the defeat in World War II,' *International Journal of Social Psychiatry*, Vol. 30, No. 3, 1984, pp. 178-187.

Chapter 8 GENERAL MACARTHUR: THE NEW EMPEROR FROM AMERICA

The defiance of the Japanese short-wave broadcasts overseas is written about in the *New York Times*, 1 September 1945, p. 2.

Some of the letters to MacArthur are reproduced in the following publications: Richard Lauterbach, 'Japs ask him favors and tell their troubles,' *Life*, 14 January 1946, pp. 4 and 7; Shukan Shincho Henshu Bu, ed., *Makkasa no Nihon, Ge*, Tokyo: Shincho Sha, 1983, pp. 45-60; Sodei Rinjiro, *Haikei Makkasa Gensui Sama*, Tokyo: Otsuki Shoten, 1985.

For the Japanese view of an authority relationship as an extension of the parent-child relationship, see Iwao Ishino 'The oyabun-kobun: A Japanese ritual kinship institution,' *American Anthropologist*, Vol. 53, 1953, pp. 695-707; John W. Bennett and Iwao Ishino, *Paternalism in the Japanese Economy: Anthropoligical Studies of Oyabun-Kobun Patterns*. Minneapolis: University of Minnesota Press, 1963; Maruyama Masao, *Gendai Seiji no Shiso to Kodo*, Enlarged Edition, Tokyo: Mirai Sha, 1964, p. 42; Asahi Shinbun, 'Oomikokoro o hotai shi sekishi no honbun tassei,' *Asahi Shinbun*, 12 August 1945, p. 1.

For the food shortage in post-war Japan, see Harold K. Johnson, *Reports of General MacArthur; Japanese Operations in the Southwest Pacific Area*, Vol. II-Part II, Washington, D.C.: U.S. Government Printing Office, 1966, p. 49.

Rumours about MacArthur's 'Japanese' background and other rumours are mentioned in John Gunther, *The Riddle of MacArthur: Japan, Korea and the Far East*, New York: Harper and Brothers, 1950, p. 226; Awaya Kentaro, *Shiryo Nihon Gendai Shi 2*, Tokyo: Otsuki Shoten, 1980, p. 250.

The imitation of chewing gum and other American behaviour are mentioned in Oshima Yukio, *Ningen Kiroku Sengo Minshu Shi*, Tokyo: Mainichi Shinbun Sha, 1976, p. 272.

For the two teenage gangsters who pretended to be Japanese Americans, see 'Jidosha goto Yamagiwa tsukamaru,' *Asahi Shinbun*, 25 September 1950, p. 2.

For other sources, see Michio Kitahara, 'Japanese responses to the defeat in World War II,' *International Journal of Social Psychiatry*, Vol. 30, No. 3, 1984, pp. 178-187.

Chapter 9 JAPANESE LITERATURE

For a social psychological discussion of 'self-hatred,' see Kurt Lewin, *Resolving Social Conflicts*, New York: Harper, 1948, Chapter 12; Michio Kitahara, 'Self-hatred among Japanese,' *Sociologus*, Vol. 37, No. 1, 1987, pp. 79-88.

Examples of the *bunmei kaika* literature are Kanagaki Robun, 'Aguranabe,' pp. 138-166, and Hattori Oga, 'Mantei Oga hen,' pp. 181-199 in *Meiji Kaikaki Bungaku Shu 1*, Tokyo: Chikuma Shobo, 1966.

Quotations from the literature after the Russo-Japanese War are; Nagai Kafu, 'Amerika monogatari,' pp. 1-344 in *Kafu Zenshu 3*, Tokyo: Iwanami Shoten, 1963, p. 220; Nagai Kafu, 'Furansu monogatari,' pp. 53-124 in *Nagai Kafu Shu*, Tokyo: Kadokawa Shoten, 1970, p. 94; Serizawa Kojiro, 'Pari ni shisu,' pp. 263-350 in *Ozaki Shiro, Ishizaka Kojiro, Serizawa Kojiro Shu*, Tokyo: Chikuma Shobo, 1971, pp. 263, 271.

Tani Jyoji's representative works are found in Tani Jyoji, *Tekisasu Mushuku, Merriken Jyappu*, Tokyo: Kawade Shobo Shin Sha, 1969.

For the literature after World War II, see Oda Makoto, 'Amerika,' pp. 5-300 in *Oda Makoto Zen Shigoto*, Vol. 2, Tokyo: Kawade Shobo Shin Sha, 1970, pp. 146-147; Ito Sei (Hitoshi), "Hino tori," pp. 230-270 in Ito Hitoshi, *Wakai Shijin no Shozo, Hino Tori*, Tokyo: Shincho Sha, 1981, pp. 231, 234.

For other sources, see Michio Kitahara, 'Psychoanalytic themes in Japanese literature,' *Psychiatric Forum*, Vol. 13, No. 1, 1985, pp. 66-75.

Chapter 10 POPULAR CULTURE IN JAPAN

The information on the first best-seller in Japan after the war was obtained from Oshima Yukio, *Ningen Kiroku Sengo Minshu Shi*, Tokyo: Mainichi Shinbun Sha, 1976, p. 272. The opinion survey in 1951 is found in Shimizu Ikutaro, ed., *Shiryo Sengo Nijyu Nen Shi*, Vol. 5, Tokyo: Nihon Hyoron Sha, 1966, p. 126.

For other sources, see Michio Kitahara, 'Popular Culture in Japan: A psychoanalytic interpretation,' *Journal of Popular culture*, Vol. 17, No. 1, 1983, pp. 103-110; Michio Kitahara, 'The Japanese and defence mechanisms,' *Journal of Psychoanalytic Anthropology*, Vol. 4, No. 4, 1981, pp. 467-479; Michio Kitahara, 'Self-hatred among Japanese,' *Sociologus*, Vol. 37, No. 1, 1987, pp. 79-88.

Chapter 11 WHITHER JAPAN?

Original sources dealing with American policies, directions, and advice regarding the future of Japan can be found in D. Clayton James, *The Years of MacArthur, Vol. III: Triumph and Disaster 1945-1964*. Boston: Houghton Mifflin, 1985. For MacArthur's desire that Japan should be 'the Switzerland of Asia,' see p. 368; For emphasis on export of finished products, see pp. 222, 228, 231, 255-256; For import restrictions, see pp. 259, 335.

For Adler's psychoanalytical thinking, see Alfred Adler, *The Practice and Theory of Individual Psychology*. New York: Harcourt, 1929.

Appendix HOW WE RESPOND TO THREAT: NINE DEFENCE MECHANISMS

For Freud's discussion of defence mechanisms, see 'The ego and the id,' pp. 1-66, Vol. 19, and 'Inhibitions, symptoms and anxiety,' pp. 75-175, Vol. 20, of *The Standard Edition of the Complete Psychological Works of Sigmund Freud*, London: Hogarth Press, 1953-1974. See also Otto Fenichel, *The Psychoanalytic Theory of Neurosis*, New York: W. W. Norton, 1945, pp. 129-167, and Ludwig Eidelberg, *Encyclopedia of Psychoanalysis*, New York: Free Press, 1968, pp. 92-96, 101-102, 106, 184-186, 201, 331-332, 366-367, 371-372, 375-376.

For Anna Freud's discussion of identification with the aggressor, see Anna Freud, *The Ego and the Mechanisms of Defence*, Revised edition, New York: International Universities Press, 1966, Chapter 9. The prisoners in concentration camps are described in Bruno Bettelheim, 'Individual and mass behaviour in extreme situations,' *Journal of Abnormal and Social Psychology*, Vol. 38, 1943, p. 417-452, and an abridged version is reprinted in T. M. Newcomb and E. L. Hartley, eds., *Readings in Social Psychology*, New York: Henry Holt & Co., 1947, pp. 628-638.

Tables

Table 1:
COMMON JAPANESE EXPRESSIONS DEALING WITH
DESIRABLE BODILY AND FACIAL CHARACTERISTICS

Expression	Approximate Meaning and Implication
Nihonjin banare no shita.	Un-Japanese looking, or with physical features unusual for a Japanese. It is meant that such a person is similar to a Westerner in appearance.
Konketsu no, or *gaijin no chi no haitta,* or *hāfu.*	Mixed blooded, or having foreign ancestry. This almost always means a Caucasian background.
Gaijin no yōna.	Similar to a foreigner. This usually means Caucasian.
Ikokufū no, or *ekizochikku na.*	Foreign or exotic. This could imply various regions of the world, but a people a Japanese thinks of are usually Caucasians rather than a people darker than the Japanese.
Hanasuji no tōta.	With a well-shaped nose.
Me no pacchiri shita.	With large and round eyes.
Futae mabuta no.	With double folded eyelids. This implies the eyes are less Oriental looking.
Horino fukai kao.	Deeply carved face (by comparing a human face to a sculpture).
Totonotta kaodachi.	Well-shaped facial features.

Table 2:

COMMON JAPANESE EXPRESSIONS DEALING WITH
UNDESIRABLE BODILY AND FACIAL CHARACTERISTICS

Expression	Approximate Meaning and Implication
Dōnaga.	With a long torso. This implies the legs are short.
Tansoku.	Short legs.
Hana pecha	Flat nose.
Pecha pai.	Flat chest.
Busu.	Unattractive, ugly woman.

Kagami o mite koi.	Look at your face in a mirror. This is an insulting expression to someone who has an ugly face but does not know how unattractive he/she is to the opposite sex.
Jibun no kao to sodan shiro.	Discuss the matter with your face. This is similar to 'Kagami o mite koi.'
Chōsenjin (Kankokujin) no yōna	Similar to a Korean. It is implied that the Koreans are ugly.
Indoneshiajin no yōna.	Similar to an Indonesian. It is implied that a person is very dark and unattractive.
Tōnan ajia kei.	A South-east Asian background. This implies a dark skin.
Nanyō jya bijin.	Can be a beauty in the South Seas. This expression is used for describing a dark-skinned unattractive woman.

Glossary

Bunmei kaika: 'Being civilised.'

Chien Han dynasty: A Chinese dynasty (202 BC — 8 AD). The official document about this dynasty includes the first written statements regarding Japan.

Daiki: A diary written by Fujiwara Yorinaga, who lived in the 12th century.

Daimyo: A land-holding military lord in pre-modern Japan.

Datsua nyuo: 'Leave Asia, join Europe.'

Defence mechanism: A psychological manipulation of thought in order to defend the self.

Denial: Refusal to admit the reality of the objective world.

Displacement: Releasing one's energy through a substitute channel.

Edo: Present-day Tokyo.

Edo Period: A period in Japanese history (1600 — 1868).

Meiji Restoration: Transfer of ruling power from the shogunate to the emperor in 1868.

Eiga Monagatari: Historical tale of the 11th century. Authorship is unknown.

Fasshonaburu: To be up to date successfully.

Fukoku kyohei: 'Enrich the country, strengthen the military.'

Gagaku: Music played in the Imperial Household and the Shinto shrines.

Gaijin: A foreigner. Usually this word implies a westerner.

Geta: Clogs.

Giri: A specific obligation to another person.

Goh: Board game using black-and-white pieces.

Haikara: State of being westernised successfully.

Haisen: Defeat in the war.

Heian period: A period in Japanese history (781 AD — 1185 AD).

Hondo kessen: 'The final and decisive battle on the main islands.'

Ichioku gyokusai: 'One hundred million Japanese will fight and die.'

Ichioku hinotama: 'One hundred million Japanese as a fireball.'

Identification with the aggressor: Placing oneself in the position of the threatening person through imagination and understanding, and looking at the world through his eyes.

Imakagami: Historical tale of the Heian period, compiled in 1170 AD. Author is unknown.

Intellectualisation: Explanation of a disturbing phenomenon by using abstract, scholarly words without involving emotion.

Isolation: Elimination of emotions and feelings from one's thought.

Kakebuton: Bedclothes.

Kakkoii: To be up to date successfully.

Kanpaku: Imperial regent for an adult emperor.

Katakana: One of the two Japanese syllabic writing systems.

Kichiku beiei: 'Devil beasts of America and Britain.'

Kimono: Traditional Japanese robe with wide sleeves.

Kojiki: The oldest chronicle in Japan compiled in 712 AD.

Kokuhon Sha: A right-wing, totalitarian organisation before and during World War II, that could be translated as 'Society for the Nation.'

Koshimaki: Women's underwear.

Kuge: A court noble.

Kyu ichi: Japanese slang for a Jew.

Manzai: Two comedians who always work as a pair on stage.

Meiji Restoration: Transfer of ruling power from the shogunate to the emperor in 1868 AD.

Meirin Kai: A right-wing, nationalist organisation before and during World War II, that could be translated as 'Association for Understanding Order.'

Ming dynasty: A Chinese dynasty (1368 AD — 1644 AD).

Mobo: A westernised man.

Moga: A westernised woman.

Nara period: A period in Japanese history (710 AD — 784 AD).

Nihon Shoki: The oldest official history of Japan, completed in 720 AD.

Nihon shugi: 'Japanism.' A form of chauvinistic nationalism advanced by such thinkers as Takayama Chogyu and Inouye Tetsujiro.

Paekche: One of the three kingdoms of early Korean history (ca. 350 AD — 663 AD). The other two were Silla and Koguryo.

Projection: Attributing one's own characteristic to another person.

Rakugo: Funny stories and jokes narrated by professional story-tellers.

Rakugoka: A professional *rakugo* story-teller.

Rationalisation: A superficial explanation which makes one's behaviour justifiable and plausible.

Reaction formation: A reversal of thought and feeling.

Regression: Going back to an earlier stage in one's life, such as an adult becoming childish.

Rojyu: A senior councillor of the *shogunate*.

Rokumeikan: The elite social club in Tokyo which was founded to promote westernisation.

Ronin: A samurai without a lord.

Saké: An alcoholic drink of fermented (not distilled) rice.

Samurai: A warrior.

Senryogun: Occupation forces.

Seppuku: Suicide by ritual disembowelment. More commonly but incorrectly known as *harakiri* in the West.

Shinchugun: Advance forces.

Shinpei: 'Divine soldier.'

Shinshu: 'Divine land.'

Shogi: Japanese chess.

Shogun: Military dictator in pre-modern Japan.

Shogunate: Military regime controlled by a *shogun*.

Shusen: End of the war.

Silla: One of the three kingdoms of ancient Korea (57 BC — 935 AD).

Sonno jyoi: 'Worship the Emperor, expel the barbarians.'

Sumato: to be up-to-date.

Sumo: Japanese wrestling.

Tairo: A position immediately below *Shogun* in the shogunate.

Tang dynasty: A Chinese dynasty (618 AD — 907 AD) with a significant impact on Japanese culture.

Tokonoma: The alcove in the room.

Tokugawa government: The shogunate of the Tokugawa family (1603-1867).

Wakon kansai: 'Japanese spirit, Chinese skill.'

Wakon yosai: 'Japanese spirit, western skill.'

Yokogaeri: A Japanese who has come back from a visit to the West.

Yoriki: A low level *samurai*, but in function analogous to a police officer.

Index